HORIZON BEYOND
ENGLISH

HORIZON BEYOND ENGLISH

초판 • 2015년 3월 1일
저자 • Lee Young-Joo, Kim Joorahn, Yang Soon-Ok
발행인 • 이성모
발행처 • 도서출판 동인 / 등록 • 제1-1599호 / 서울시 종로구 명륜동 2가 237 아남주상복합Ⓐ 118호
TEL • (02) 765-7145 / FAX • (02) 765-7165
E-mail • dongin60@chollian.net / Homepage • donginbook.co.kr

ISBN 978-89-5506-644-9   13740

정가: 13,000원

HORIZON BEYOND
ENGLISH

Lee Young-Joo, Kim Joorahn, Yang Soon-Ok

도서출판 동인

Table of Contents

International Affairs

01 Why Korea Should Embrace Multiculturalism

by Anwar Kemal

The UN Committee on the Elimination of Racial Discrimination recommended on Aug. 17 that South Korea acknowledge it is now a multiethnic society and make laws against racial discrimination. UNCERD said unrealistic emphasis on and excessive pride in the ethnic homogeneity of Korea is no longer in the national interest. The recommendation was important news and marked a watershed in Korean society.

The Chosun Ilbo spoke via phone and e-mail to Anwar Kemal, the expert who served as country rapporteur for South Korea. He said Korea should avoid using racially discriminatory expressions like "pure blood" and "mixed blood." The Pakistani diplomat was appointed to the four-year term of rapporteur this year.

— *Why did UNCERD urge Korea to legislate laws against racial discrimination several times in the report?*

We recognize Korea's efforts to eliminate racial discrimination, but more is needed. We want Korea to legislate an anti-racial discrimination law in line with the UN standard. The Korean parliament should define what racial discrimination is: that is the first thing to do to eliminate discrimination against alien workers, foreign spouses of Korean people and children from multi-ethnic families. The Korean Constitution doesn't ban racial discrimination in detail.

— *How is South Korea doing compared to other countries?*

Korea has achieved amazing economic growth for the past 40 years. However, it has not opened itself to foreign workers sufficiently compared to developed countries like the U.S., Germany and Britain. Among developed countries, Sweden is the country that has made the most remarkable achievement in removing racial discrimination. A female immigrant from Burundi, Nyamko Sabuni, is the minister for integration and gender equality in Sweden.

— *Koreans have identified themselves with the nation for a long time. In Korea, nationalism was a means for promoting social integration and resisting foreign invasions.*

I know. But now Korea is an industrialized country. It is not a weak country facing threats from foreign forces. Also, nationalism in this day and age is not based on ethnic homogeneity. Take the example of Brazil and the U.S. They are multi-racial countries. But their people are very patriotic.

— *Why is it so important to avoid using discriminatory expressions like "pure blood" and "mixed blood"?*

Many people find them insulting and those expressions are not scientific. A

DNA research leader like Korea shouhn't use such expressions. All people's blood is the same.

— *Is it inevitable for Korea to become a multi-racial society?*

Korea has the world's lowest birthrate. It will see its population drastically decrease 10-20 years from now. The number of money earners will decrease, and instead the number of pension recipients and retirees will increase. Korea is already suffering from a serious shortage of manual workers. The nation's economy will be hit hard by the lack of labor forces unless it accepts immigrant workers.

— *Which one is better, assimilating foreign workers for social integration or respecting their culture and accepting the coexistence of heterogeneous cultures?*

All foreign workers should be encouraged to learn Korean. They also need to have an orientation about Korean culture, labor ethics and etiquette. But it is unwise to keep them from preserving their own culture. It does no harm when foreign workers preserve their culture. Rather, it can help social stability.

READING COMPREHENSION

■ Indicate if each statement is true (T) or false (F) according to the reading.

1. _____ Anwar Kemal works for S. Korean government.

2. _____ UNCERD disregards S. Korea's treatment toward foreigners.

3. _____ It is preferable to assimilating foreign workers for social integration.

4. _____ Unrealistic emphasis on and excessive pride in the ethnic

   homogeneity of Korea is in the national interest.

■ Discuss the following questions with your classmates.

1. Why do Koreans emphasis on nationalism?

2. Why should we consider about Multiculturalism?

3. Do you think Korea will become *a multi-racial society*?

   If no, why not? If yes, what should we do?

4. What are your thoughts about other ethnics working in Korea?

02 China Waiting for Democracy

by Jela De Francheschi

Many analysts say China is disproving a long-standing assumption in the West that democracy follows economic liberalization. They say China's rapid economic growth has helped its communist regime bolster its political legitimacy and stalled much-needed democratic reforms in China.

Ever since Deng Xiaoping launched major economic liberalization in the late 1970s, inaugurating an era of extraordinary economic growth in China, many Western observers argued that political reform would follow.

Bruce Bueno de Mesquita, Chairman of the Department of Politics at New York University says the assumption that economic growth produces an educated, capitalist middle class that demands control over its own fate has not been the case in China. He points out, "When Deng announced his economic reforms, the standard view in the West was that China was quickly going to become a different, democratic kind of country. It's now 27 years since those reforms were put into place, and there is no evidence of any meaningful change in the way governance is done in China."

Professor Bueno de Mesquita adds that authoritarian governments around the world, including China's, are showing that they can reap the benefits of economic development while resisting any pressure to relax their power. He notes, "What a lot of autocrats have figured out is that prosperity can be a substitute for freedom and democracy, and that the big threat to them is not promoting economic growth, promoting good health care, having reasonably good literacy rates, because all of those things are beneficial to productivity. What is harmful to them is people having the right to freely assemble, a transparent government, a free press. It is very cheap to suppress those freedoms while promoting economic progress, so that people are fed and happy and don't worry so much about turning their governments out of power."

Stifling the internet

According to some estimates, China is the world's second-largest economy, after the United States. Its robust economic expansion has been fueled mainly by foreign investment. An increasing number of foreign businesses are operating in China, which is often called the "workshop of the world." More than 44,000 foreign operations, worth about $60 billion, were set up last year alone.

U.S. businesses are especially attracted to China's technology market, the fastest growing in the world. There are an estimated 110 million Chinese Internet users and that number will likely skyrocket to 250 million by the end of the decade.

But China monitors its citizens' Internet activity, blocks information from websites, and frequently jails those who are accused of what it deems subversive cyber-action. And, high-tech giants like Microsoft, Google, Yahoo, and Cisco Systems have to comply with Chinese censorship laws in order to do business there. They have been vociferously accused of aiding Beijing's crackdown on dissent.

Clyde Prestowitz, President of the Economic Strategy Institute in Washington and author of the book, *Three Billion New Capitalists: The Great Shift of Wealth and Power to the East* says American corporations often are caught in situations beyond their control.

He argues, "When Congress passed legislation to bring China into the World Trade Organization and when Congress agreed to give China most favored nation treatment [i.e. most favored nation trading status], it was taking steps to encourage U.S. companies to do business with China. Every body knew that we were not dealing with a democracy. Everybody knew that the Chinese leadership had different views about handling information than we did. The companies obviously see China as a big opportunity. And if they are not there, other competitors will be. But it does call into question the extent to which global companies can be co-opted by authoritarian governments."

The Globalization Game

After years of complaints by free speech and human rights advocates, the United states Congress is considering new rules to govern overseas operations of American internet companies. But trade expert Clyde Prestowitz contends that loosening Beijing's grip on the way foreign corporations do business in China requires an international effort. He adds that pressure is building within China itself and notes that a number of high-level former Chinese officials recently urged President Hu Jintao to ease censorship.

Analyst Clyde Prestowitz says, "Because there are important people in China who understand the significance of freedom of speech, there is a lot of room for the U.S and other Western and Asian figures—Koreans, Japanese, and others—to play a role as well. They can sit down and talk to the Chinese and say, 'we are playing this globalization game and here is how the game really has to be played.'"

Many observers argue that despite the regime's efforts to gain more legitimacy through economic success, pressure for democratic reform will only grow in China.

Minxin Pei, Director of the China Program at the Carnegie Endowment for international Peace in Washington, says there are powerful transformational trends underway. He contends, "Rapid economic growth is producing two things: enormous social strain and instability that will build up pressure for reform; and secondly, economic growth is creating the right conditions—a middle class, private property, and interconnectedness with the international community—that will, in the long run, be good for democracy."

"Foreign companies," says analyst Minxin Pei, "are further diminishing communist control in China. They compete," he says, "against a state-owned company, so they are reducing the strength of the state-owned economy. And that will weaken, in the long run, the Communist Party's monopoly over economic power. Second, they are bringing the best managerial practices, which emphasizes competition, open-mindedness, and meritocracy that again will increase pressure on the system to reform and create a much more liberal culture."

Many critics and defenders of the role Western business interests play in China agree that the country's eventual democratization is inevitable. They add

that with China's joining of the global democratic movement, roughly two-thirds of the world's population could, for the first time, live in free societies grounded in universal democratic norms.

READING COMPREHENSION

■ Indicate if each statement is true (T) or false (F) according to the reading.

1. _____ Western countries have long assumed that economic

prosperity in China would be followed by political change.

2. _____ Authoritarian governments have learned that they can

provide economic prosperity without losing their power.

3. _____ Economic growth can lead to democracy in China.

4. _____ China will not likely become a democracy one day.

5. _____ Chinese are happy as long as they are heartily fed.

■ Discuss the following questions with your classmates.

1. According to the essay, China's economy is fuelled by foreign business, but at the same time, what do they do in the action of letting the steam off from China?

2. What is the difference between China and Korea in the sense of current economy situation?

3. Do you think that democracy is inevitable in China?

4. What aspects of Chinese life style can you compare with Koreans'?

5. What is your opinion about Chinese internet activity control?

03 Asia Goes Crazy over Korean Pop Culture

by Claudia Blume

The hottest thing in Asian pop culture these days is South Korea. The so-called Korean wave covers the craze for South Korean TV dramas, movies, and pop singers—but increasingly also for fashion, cosmetics, and electronics.

The Korean drama *Jewel in the palace* clocked up record television ratings in China, Hong Kong, and Taiwan last year. Even Chinese President Hu Jin Tao admitted to being a fan of the historical drama about a cook at Korea's royal court. The show's actors have become mega stars across Asia.

South Korea has been exporting movies and TV dramas since the late 1990s. Many Asian TV networks initially bought them because the glossy productions were comparatively cheap. But audiences from China to the Philippines soon got hooked.

Lisa Leung is assistant professor of cultural studies at Hong Kong's Lingnan University. She says one of the reasons for the dramas' strong appeal is that, unlike Western productions, they are culturally close to Asian viewers.

"Audiences can not only identify with the skin color, the hair color, the similar faces and looks of Korean actors and actresses but also the kind of values expressed in these TV dramas," she explained. "More to the point, the kind of stress on familial values, the filial piety, the love between siblings, and friendship and all these elements that might make Korean television dramas so popular in Asia."

South Korean pop stars, like the singer BOA, have also achieved cult status in many Asian countries. One young woman in Hong Kong looks for magazines and posters featuring her favorite pop star, the South Korean singer and actor Rain.

"I like him, I'm his big fan," she said, "He dances great and he sings great. And his performance in the drama is good as well."

The popularity of South Korean films and music has led to a veritable craze for everything Korean across Asia.

Hong Kong street markets sell traditional Korean robes to children and some brides in China are wearing them for wedding photos.

Learning Korean has become increasingly popular in many Asian countries, as have Korean food, fashion, and cosmetics, Ms. Leung says in China the craze has even meant more people undergoing plastic surgery, as she noticed during a research trip last year.

"I found that there were more and more younger girls and also older women wanting to go through plastic surgery," she said. "They would be visiting these hospitals which stress this kind of Korean-style cosmetic technology. This is not too much of a question of wanting to look more Korean, but I think in mainland China the audience might have been affected by Korean TV dramas and that they want to look more beautiful."

Ms. Leung says advertisements featuring South Korean idols have resulted in increased sales for the country's products, such as Samsung mobile phones or LG electrical appliances.

Shim Doo-bo, A South Korean, is assistant professor of communications and news media at Singapore's National University. He says Koreans living overseas have profited from the popularity of their country's cultural exports–like the South Korean housewives he interviewed in Singapore.

"They reported to me that after the immense popularity of Korean television dramas and films they feel that they are better treated by local Singaporean people," said Shim Doo-bo.

In many parts of Asia, Korea has become a byword for cool. South Koreans have coined a new word to describe the phenomenon: Hallyu, meaning "Korean wave."

Mr. Shim says his country has not been slow to cash in on the craze.

"Many regional governments within Korea have built up theme parks based on the characters of Korean dramas and films and the image of [South] Korea of a country which used to be known to other countries for labor strikes or student demonstration strikes for democracy is slowly moving to cool or fashionable or dynamic," he said. "So that recently officially the [South] Korean government

inaugurated a campaign of so-called dynamic Korea as its catchphrase for the tourist industry."

As Asian tourists are now visiting South korea specifically to see the locations where popular dramas are shot, the government has organized events with famous entertainers and launched a multilingual web site with information on movies and TV dramas, actors, and filming locations.

The Korean wave is a point of national pride for South Korea. After having been colonized or overshadowed by its neighbors, Japan and China, for centuries, the country finally has the chance to outdo them on the cultural stage.

But Hallyu has also boosted South Korea's economy. In 2004, the export of film and television programs along with tourism and merchandising generated revenues totaling nearly $2 billion.

READING COMPREHENSION

■ Indicate if each statement is true (T) or false (F) according to the reading.

1. _____ South Korea has been exporting movies and TV dramas since

   the late 1980s.

2. _____ Shim Doo-bo says Korea has been slow to cash in on the craze.

3. _____ The explosive popularity of the Korean drama Jewel in the palace,

   which has sparked a craze across Asia for all things Korean.

4. _____ Hallyu includes not only TV shows, pop singers, and movies,

   but also fashion, cosmetics, and electronics.

5. _____ South Koreans have coined a new word to describe the

   phenomenon : Hallyu

■ Discuss the following questions with your classmates.

1. According to the essay, "Korean" becomes byword for cool and fantastic.

   Do you agree with that? If not, why?

2. What can you think of boosting Korean economy using Hallyu?

3. What is the purpose of the campaign, "Dynamic Korea"?

4. Share with your thoughts who coined "Hallyu"?

5. Do you still think Hallyu affects on Korean ecomony?

Science, Health & Environment

04 Researchers Identify New Targets to Disrupt HIV Lifecycle

by Art Chimes

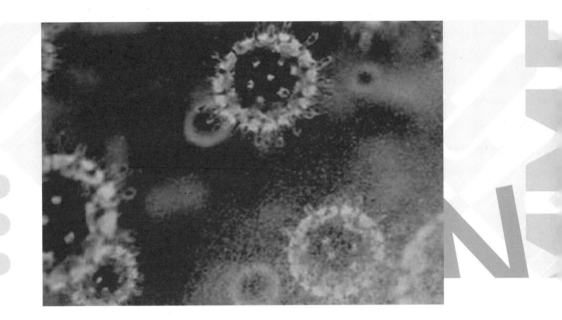

In what is being hailed as a major step in the fight against HIV/AIDS, US researchers have identified 273 proteins that are key to reproduction of the virus that cause AIDS. As we hear from VOA science correspondent Art Chimes, that gives scientists many potential new targets for drugs to disrupt the sophisticated lifecycle of the virus.

Publication of this new study promises to give researchers more avenues to follow as they look for better ways to stop the AIDS epidemic.

"The set of proteins will provide a lot of insight into how the virus actually functions. And people may be able to use that information to somehow circumvent the virus. But the other way you can look at it is that now there are more targets. They're potential targets."

Stephen Elledge of Harvard Medical School, is the lead author of the paper describing the discovery, which was published Thursday online in Science Express.

HIV has little genetic material of its own, so when it infects a cell, it hijacks the cell's genetic code to reproduce. This new study identifies some of the cell proteins the virus uses in that process.

Speaking in a Science magazine podcast, Elledge said current anti-AIDS drugs generally focus on the virus itself. "But the problem is that HIV is a highly mutable virus, so it can change the target of the drug so that it no longer binds the drug that well." Which is why Elledge focused on human proteins. Of the 273 he identified as being essential to HIV reproduction, only thirty-six were previously known.

Leading AIDS researchers hailed Elledge's work, HIV co-discoverer, Robert Gallo, called it "terrific." Dr. Anthony Fauci, head of the US National Institute of Allergy and Infectious Diseases, described it as "elegant science," but he told The New York Times that it's too soon to tell if this laboratory discovery will actually prove useful in treating patients.

Elledge also admits there could be side-effects to any treatments developed using his discovery.

"And the downside, the potential downside, is that if the organism–us–needs that particular protein, [then] if you inhibit it, you might get sick. And of course, that's true for any drug. If anyone finds a drug target and they decide they're going to make a drug that inhibits it, it has to be tested on people to see how people tolerate having that pathway reduced."

To find the 273 proteins that are part of the HIV life cycle, Elledge and his

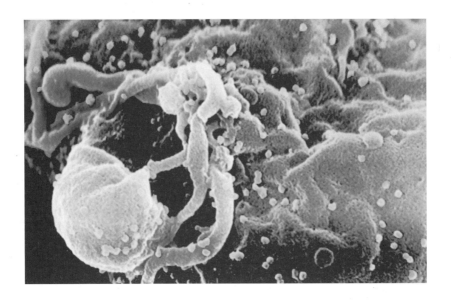

colleagues screened thousands of possibilities using a technique honored with a Nobel Prize a year ago, RNA interference, which can be used to effectively shut down one gene at a time within a cell. Then the researchers infected the cell with HIV to see if the virus could reproduce.

"And we did this for ever 20,000 human proteins, all the known, currently known proteins to figure out which ones might be important," Elledge explains. "We wanted to cover everything, we wanted to leave no stone unturned to see what the list looked like. And that's how we did it."

Stephen Elledge, of Harvard Medical School and the Howard Hughes Medical Institute, says the same approach could be used to find targets in the fight against other virus infections as well.

■ Indicate if each statement is true (T) or false (F) according to the reading.

1. _____ "The scientists leave no stone unturned in their search for a

   cure for cancer" means that they were negligent to find the cure

   for cancer.

2. _____ Researchers know of 213 human proteins that are essential to

   HIV reproduction.

3. _____ Stephen Elledge and his colleagues used RNA interference to

   screen more than 200,000 human proteins.

4. _____ According to this essay, everyone welcomed Ellege's findings.

5. _____ In the future, we will get the gene treatment at the hospital.

■ Discuss the following questions with your classmates.

1. Is this the first time for you to recognize the difference of HIV and AIDS?

2. How does HIV virus infect the cell?

3. Do you think it is applicable for Dr. Ellege's findings to virus related dieses

   in the future?

4. How do you prevent AIDS?

5. Is HIV virus hereditary?

05 Trouble on the Table

by David Bjerklie

Some people find genetically altered superfoods hard to swallow.

What do you get when you cross a chicken with an apple? A daffodil with rice? A flounder with a tomato? These aren't jokes waiting for a punch line. Believe it or not, combinations like these may make their way to your dinner table. There's a brave new world of agriculture that has some people excited about new superfoods. Others are very nervous.

For thousands of years, farmers improved their crops by patiently crossbreeding plants that have good traits. They would take pollen from the sweetest melon plants and add it to the flowers of plants that produced the biggest melons to create new plants with melons that are both sweet and big. But crossbreeding doesn't always work. Even when it does, it can take decades to get good results.

Now, thanks to advances in genes science, there are amazing shortcuts. Genes are the instructions inside cells that help determine what a living thing looks like: its size, its shape and countless other traits. Using the new tools of genetic engineering, scientists can take a gene from one living thing and put it directly into another plant or animal. That way, says John Mount, professor of agriculture at the University of Tennessee, "you can make changes more precisely in a much shorter period of time."

Here's how it works. First, scientists identify a gene that controls a desirable trait—for example, a protein in an Arctic flounder that helps the fish thrive in frigid waters. The scientists then use chemicals to cut and paste the flounder gene into the genes of tomato cells in a test tube. The cells grow into a tomato plant. Then the plant is tested to see if the fish gene still works. Do its tomatoes resist the cold? Yes, they do!

Scientists believe the new techniques can create crops that are pest-proof, disease resistant and more nutritious. Researchers are working on rice that has an extra boost of vitamin A from a daffodil gene. The rice could help prevent blindness, even death, for millions of kids who don't get enough vitamin A in their diet.

Are we making monster food?

Not everybody is convinced that pumping up our food with foreign genes is a good idea. Many people say these genetically modified, or GM, foods may end up harming the environment and humans. They fear that plants with new genes forced into them will accidently crossbreed with wild plants and create pesticide-resistant superweeds. They also say GM foods could carry genes that trigger allergies or other side effects. Already, there's evidence that some GM corn crops may be harmful to the caterpillars that turn into monarch butterflies. "We are rushing headlong into a new technology," warns Ronnie Cummins of the Organic Consumers Association. "We are courting disaster if we don't look before we leap." Nearly half the U.S. corn and soybean crops are now genetically modified. Health concerns are growing. Many groups are demanding that GM foods be labeled. Last year public worry forced the Gerber and Heinz companies to stop using GM ingredients in baby foods. Just last month Frito Lay announced that its snacks would be free of GM ingredients. Companies are seeing that GM foods can be bad for business, even if they haven't been proved to be bad for health.

So far, GM foods haven't harmed anyone. Most genetic researchers believe that if troubles do crop up, they will be manageable. "We're not talking killer tomatoes here," says Norm Ellstrand, a University of California geneticist. As the battles go on, will we continue to see GM food on our tables? "I hope so," answers Allison Snow, an ecologist at Ohio State University. "Even though I have concerns, I think it would be silly not to use this technology. We just have to use it wisely."

Did you know? Genetically Modified Food (GM food)

A genetically modified food is a food product derived in whole or part from a genetically modified organism (GMO) such as a crop plant, animal or microbe such as yeast. Genetically modified foods have been available since the 1990s. The principle ingredients of GM foods currently available are derived from genetically modified soybean, maize and canola.

Some governments have a very strong mutual disagreement over the labeling

and traceability requirements for GM food products. For example, the European Union and Japan require labeling and traceability while regulatory agencies in the United States do not believe these requirements are necessary.

Benefits and risks The majority of commercially available crops have an agronomic advantage like herbicide tolerance or insect resistance. These traits offer major benefits to the consumer from these traits: GM crops have shown to contribute to significantly reduced greenhouse gas emissions from agricultural practices. This reduction results from decreased fuel use, about 1.8 billion liters in the past nine years. In 2004, their reduction was equivalent to eliminating more than 10 billion kg of carbon dioxide from the atmosphere.

Controversies surrounding GM foods and crops commonly focus on human and environmental safety, labeling and consumer choice, intellectual property rights, ethics, food security, poverty reduction, and environmental conservation. Although no major health hazards have come to light since GM food was introduced 12 years ago, some fear for the long term health risks which GM could pose, or that the risks of GM have not yet been adequately investigated.

READING COMPREHENSION

■ Indicate if each statement is true (T) or false (F) according to the reading.

1. _____ GM foods and crops commonly focus on human and environment.

2. _____ The principal ingredients of GM foods currently available are

derived from genetically modified soybean and canola.

3. _____ Last year public worry forced the Gerber Companies to use

GM ingredients.

4. _____ For thousands of years, farmers improved their crops by patiently

crossbreeding plants that have good traits.

5. _____ GM food is mostly welcomed in Japan.

■ Discuss the following questions with your classmates.

1. What is your opinion on GM food?

2. Would you rather eat GM food?

3. Have you noticed GM food at your local groceries?

4. How do the scientists make GM food?

5. What are the advantages of GM food?

06   One Bad Bug

by Claudia Wallis

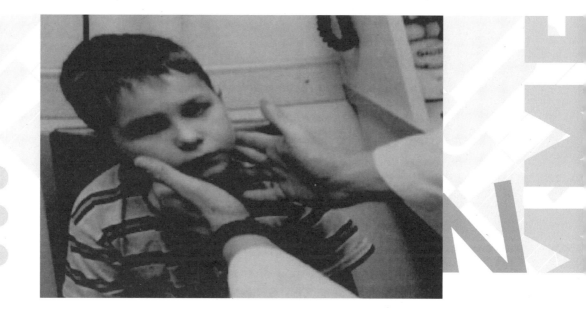

The influenza virus is off to a roaring start every winter. Will the flu bug bite you?

There's nothing gradual about the flu: it slams you like a hammer. One minute you're feeling fine. Next thing you know, you're shivering, you're burning up, then shivering again. In minutes, your legs turn to jelly and your body aches in places that have never hurt before. "Influenza has such a sudden onset that people can sometimes say, 'It hit me at exactly 9 last night,'" says Dr. Carolyn Bridges, an expert on influenza at the Centers for Disease Control(CDC) in Atlanta, Georgia. But whether the flu strikes at night or on the bus to schol, there's just one thing a victim wants to do: collapse into bed.

Right now there's a whole lot of collapsing going on. Flu season lasts from November through April, and this year's bug is a doozy. "I'm sending home about twice as many kids as I usually do." says Jane Allen, a school nurse in Lubbock, Texas. Thirty-one states have big outbreaks of flu. Clinics and hospital emergency rooms are bursting with feverish, coughing, miserable patients. "My nose is so stuffy, I just want to cut it off!" groans Nekedria Clark, a student at New York's Pace University.

It's too soon to say just how bad this flu season will be. Certainly, it won't compare to the famous epidemic of 1918, when influenza struck 1 out of 4 Americans and killed 20 million worldwide. But even in an ordinary year, about 1 in 10 Americans gets the flu. And as you may have noticed from all those empty desks at school, kids are most frequent victims.

Tiny Viruses, Big Miseries

Like the common cold, influenza is caused by a tiny virus. Several million flu bugs could fit on the period at the end of this sentence. The virus spreads from person to person on the tiny droplets produced by a sneeze or a cough.

Once inside the body, flu viruses settle into the delicate cells that line the lungs, nose and throat. There the sneaky invaders steal the body's own building tools to create billions of copies of themselves. These viruses quickly spread into more cells. Most awful flu symptoms - fever, runny nose, body aches - are caused not by the virus itself but by your body's attempt to get rid of it. A healthy person can fight off the flu in three to five days, though a cough and tired feeling can last two more weeks.

Doctors believe the damage done by the flu virus makes it easier for other germs to attack, including the bacteria that cause ear infections and pneumonia. The one-two punch of flu followed by pneumonia is the sixth leading cause of death in the U.S. Nine out of 10 of these deaths occur in elderly people. The lesson for people of any age: if you aren't getting better after four or five days of the flu, or if you get better then get worse, see a doctor.

Medical Weapons

Every year lots of flu victims are seeking relief with drugs that target viruses. Two new ones–Relenza and Tamiflu – have been heavily advertised on TV. They don't cure the flu, but they can make it a little less awful.

Doctors recommend that people who are old, or people of any age with heart or lung problems like asthma, get an annual shot of the flu vaccine. Because flu viruses change all the time, a new vaccine must be prepared each your to protect against the latest versions. Right now a medical team at the CDC and others in Britain, Japan and Australia are busy studying the current crop of viruses to develop next year's shot.

Should healthy kids get the vaccine? "That's something to talk over with a doctor," says Bridges. The main side effect, she notes "is a sore arm." If that sounds bad, stay tuned. Researchers are developing a new kind of vaccine that's nothing to sniff at. It enters the body the same way the bad old virus does: through your nose!

The Flu and You

It begins with a runny nose, a cough or a sore throat. It usually ends with a headache, fever, exhaustion and aches from head to toe. It's the flu, which is the common name for the illness caused by a tiny germ known as the influenza virus. This year, people are talking about a type of influenza called bird flu. Here are a few answers to common questions about flu.

Q : Who gets the flu?

A : Each year, up to 20% of the U.S. population gets sick from this bad bug. That's 60 million people, so chances are good that the flu will hit someone you know this year. Most feel miserable for a week or two and then get better. The flu can be deadly, however, for babies, elderly people and anyone who is already sick with a serious, long-term disease.

Q : How do people catch the flu?

A : The flu can be very contagious. People spread it before they even feel sick and for a week after they get sick. The virus is spread in tiny drops of moisture that are sprayed into the air when we cough or sneeze.

Q : Can flu be prevented?

A : Yes. A vaccine can protect a person from coming down with the flu. But because the flu virus is constantly changing, scientists must create a new vaccine formula each year. Not knowing exactly what kind of flu to protect against can delay the process of making the right vaccine.

Q : Can flu be treated?

A : Yes. A new drug known as Tamiflu is the best treatment for flu patients. But it has to be taken in the first two days after catching the flu.

Q : What is bird flu?

A : Right now, this variety of flu is found mostly in chickens and ducks raised by

farmers in a few countries, such as China, Vietnam, Turkey and Romania. There is no bird flu in the United States. Public-health experts worry that if this type of flu virus changes and becomes easier for people to catch, it could cause an outbreak much worse than regular flu.

Q : What is being done to prevent bird flu from infecting humans?

A : In countries where bird flu has been found, medical officials are testing flocks and destroying sick birds. In the U.S., the President and the Congress are trying to prepare the country in case there is ever a flu emergency. There is a plan to stockpile flu vaccines and medicines.

READING COMPREHENSION

■ Indicate if each statement is true (T) or false (F) according to the reading.

1. _____ Women are the most frequent victims of the flu.

2. _____ If you are not getting better after few days of the flu, take more
rest is the best thing to do.

3. _____ Hunger is the one of the symptom that our body is trying to get
rid of influenza virus.

4. _____ Influenza is caused by a tiny virus.

5. _____ Influenza begins with a runny nose, a cough or a sore throat.

■ Discuss the following questions with your classmates.

1. How does the flu spread from person to person?

2. Why must a new flu vaccine be prepared each year?

3. Did you ever catch the flu or serious cold?

4. How would you prevent flu?

5. What is the role of Center for Disease Control?

07 Gamers: Image and Reality

by Casey Malarcher, Andrea Janzen, Adam Worcester

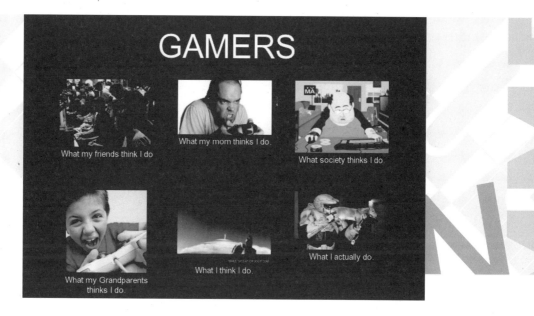

Video games have become very popular. There are numerous games for the personal computer. Additionally, game systems like the Sony Playstation and the Xbox can be found in many homes. As video games have become more popular and sophisticated, they have influenced popular culture. The character of Lara Croft from the game, *Tomb Raider*, is well known even to people who have never played the game. There have been several movies based on video games, *Tomb Raider* included. Obviously, the video game industry is highly profitable, and the designers of a successful game can become very rich. Of course, what this means is that there are many people buying and playing video games. What kinds of people are they?

There are many stereotypes about gamers. The first one is that most gamers are males. Another stereotype about gamers is that they are not interesting or attractive people. According to this view, gamers are mostly fat because they always play games instead of exercising. Even if they are not fat, they are still unhealthy because they rarely go outside or do anything active. Another part of this image is that gamers are ugly. They play games because it is impossible for them to find girlfriends. Not only are they ugly, but they are also boring. Gamers have no interests outside games, so games are all that they can talk about, besides computers. Further, this image of gamers implies they are antisocial. They do not know how to communicate with other people. This is the main reason that they play games. Gamers spend all of their time alone with their computers, and they only connect with other people through the Internet, where they can pretend to be different people. This sort of communication is not real, since gamers would never be able to talk the same way with people in the normal world.

The most negative stereotype about gamers is that they possibly have emotional problems. Many video games are violent, so gamers might be influenced by that violence. They may start to feel that it is OK to use violence in real life. Further, gamers spend too much time in the false worlds of their games. The result is that they can no longer recognize the real world. They may come to believe that they are characters in a game. The result of this could be violence or destruction of property, either real or through computer hacking.

Of course, these views are only stereotypes. There may be some gamers that fit the negative stereotype. However, a recent study about gamers was conducted in the United States by the Pew Internet and American Life Project. This research involved a survey of 1,162 college students across the United States. The

survey found that most gamers are the same as normal people. According to the survey, both gamers and non-gamers spent the same amount of time doing different kinds of activities, like studying and exercising. Gamers did not spend all their time playing games. They did not spend all their time alone, either. Most of the gamers in the survey lived normal lives and had normal friends. For them, gaming was a social activity. These gamers were unlikely to commit violence against others. Finally, the survey found that just as many women as men played video games.

According to this survey, at least, gaming has become a normal hobby, like any other, and as is the case with many other stereotypes, the stereotypical image of gamers does not seem to match with reality.

READING COMPREHENSION

■ Indicate if each statement is true (T) or false (F) according to the reading.

1. _____ For several years, video games have become more popular and
   sophisticated.

2. _____ The stereotyped image of a gamer is a man who is ugly and fat.

3. _____ For some people, gamers are thought to be very social.

4. _____ Some people think that gamers possibly have emotional problems.

5. _____ Research indicates that gamers were likely to commit violence
   against others.

■ Discuss the following questions with your classmates.

1. What are the stereotyped images of the gamers according to the reading
   passage? What are the stereotypes of your own about the gamers?

2. What do you think are the advantages and disadvantages of playing video
   games?

3. How many hours a day do you spend playing computer or video games?
   Do you think that is enough? Why or why not?

08 Ideas About Beauty

by Casey Malarcher, Andrea Janzen, Adam Worcester

Researchers have collected convincing evidence that people tend to rate beauty in much the same way. Groups even from different cultures do not really show that much difference in judging the main factors of beauty. However, researchers do not agree on whether the factors which influence how most people judge beauty come from genetics or culture.

Devendra Singh, a psychologist at the University of Texas at Austin, conducted an experiment in 1993 to find out if different men found different female body shapes attractive. Dr. Singh gave drawings of different female body shapes to a variety of men and asked them to choose the most attactive body shape. Even though men came from a wide range of cultural backgrounds, they all tended to rate the "hourglass" body shape as the most attractive. In fact, Dr. Singh found that any woman whose waist is 70 percent as wide as her hips is judged as attractive by most men no matter how big the woman is overall. Body shape, not weight, seemed to be viewed as the critical factor for attractiveness by men in this survey.

Dr. Singh explained this result from the perspective of evolution. Women who develop an hourglass shape have a relatively higher level of estrogen, a female hormone, than women who do not have this body shape. Because estrogen levels also influence fertility, men may subconsciously view a woman with an hourglass figure as a good candidate for producing children. Therefore, according to Dr. Singh, the men who choose these types of women have the potential for having more children. Over time, evolution would favor men who have inherited genes from their fathers which influence the selection of this type of "fertile" woman.

Douglas Yu, a biologist at Imperial College in London, disagrees with Dr. Singh's hypothesis. Dr. Yu thinks that culture, especially culture developed through exposure to mass entertainment and advertising, has had the largest influence on how men judge beauty. In order to test his theory, Dr. Yu traveled to southeast Peru to interview men in an isolated community far from the reach of modern television, movies, and magazines. Through his own survey, Dr. Yu found that the men in this isolated community preferred heavier women with a wider waist than the body shape preferred by the men in Dr. Singh's study. Because this small community has lived apart from western mass communication, their own culture has not been influenced by outside standards of beauty.

In order to check the reliability of his study, Dr. Yu surveyed two other groups of men from this same community. The second and third groups surveyed

by Dr. Yu had more exposure to western entertainment and advertising. The results of these later surveys showed that as men from this isolated community came into contact with western movies and magazines, their standards of beauty began to change more toward the western standard of beauty. Dr. Yu concluded from these findings that even if evolution played a part in men's selection of mates, cultural influences are more powerful in the end and work faster in changing men's standards.

With both satellite communication and the Internet flooding every corner of the world with images and information from almost every culture, it is becoming harder and harder to find isolated communities. Soon it may be impossible to prove which side is correct in the genetics versus culture debate simply because there will be no uninfluenced groups left to ask.

■ Indicate if each statement is true (T) or false (F) according to the reading.

1. _____ Researchers agree that only genetics have a greater influence on how most people judge beauty.

2. _____ The men in Dr. Singh's experiment rate breast and hip size more important than weight.

3. _____ Douglas Yu traveled to Africa to interview men who had no exposure to the mass media.

4. _____ According to Dr. Singh's survey, men tend to view a woman with an hourglass figure as a fertile woman.

5. _____ The mass media have little influence on men's standards of beauty.

■ Discuss the following questions with your classmates.

1. When you meet someone for the first time, what do you usually tend to notice about him or her?

2. Do you focus on his or her physical attractiveness, body size and weight? What is your standard of beauty?

3. Do you believe that a person's physical appearance is more important than his or her personality? If not, what do you think is the most important thing in your life?

09   Answers About Ebola

TFK answers some key questions about this serious disease

by Nicoletta Richardson

You may have heard a lot about Ebola lately. A new outbreak of this disease has spread through the West African countries of Liberia, Guinea, Sierra Leone, and, most recently, Nigeria. Researchers think this outbreak began in December 2013. Since then, nearly 2,000 people have become infected with the Ebola virus, and more than 1,000 have died from it. Scientists and doctors are working to stop its spread, and to care for the people who are infected.

In late July, two American aid workers in West Africa became infected with

Ebola. They were brought back to the United States for treatment. Many Americans are wondering if the virus could become a problem here. Experts say there is no need to worry. Read on to find out why, and to learn the answers to some other common questions about Ebola.

What is Ebola?

Ebola, or Ebola hemorrhagic fever (Ebola HF), is a contagious and life-threatening disease. It affects humans and other primates, including monkeys, gorillas, and chimpanzees. Ebola gets its name from the Ebola River in the Democratic Republic of Congo. The disease was first reported in a village on the river in 1976.

What are the symptoms of Ebola?

The early symptoms include fever, headache, joint and muscle aches, weakness, chills, difficulty breathing, and a sore throat. As the disease becomes worse, diarrhea, vomiting, and bleeding inside and outside of the body may start to occur. The first signs of infection can appear anywhere from 2 to 21 days after exposure to the virus.

How does Ebola spread?

Experts are not sure how an Ebola outbreak starts. The virus spreads from direct contact with bodily fluids including blood, saliva, sweat, and urine of infected people and animals. Animals in Africa believed to carry Ebola include other primates, fruit bats, porcupines, and forest antelope.

Doctors and nurses are at a high risk of infection because they come into physical contact with Ebola patients. Also, family members who care for infected relatives are more likely to catch the disease, especially if they don't wear proper protective equipment, such as gloves and masks.

Can Ebola be treated?

Yes. Most people who become infected with Ebola need special care in a hospital. Treatment includes making sure they get plenty of liquids and oxygen, keeping their blood pressure steady, and addressing symptoms and complications as they come up. Patients also need to be kept from the public to help prevent the disease from spreading.

There is no cure for Ebola, but doctors are working on a vaccine to prevent it. Some experimental drugs have been developed to treat the disease. They have been effective in animals, but have not yet been approved for testing on humans.

Are we safe in the United States?

Yes. There have been no reported cases of Ebola spreading to the U.S. The two American aid workers who recently became infected with Ebola in West Africa were flown back to the U.S. and hospitalized immediately. While Ebola is contagious, it is not as contagious as the flu. Special medical planes and vehicles were used to transport the infected patients to prevent the disease from spreading.

Can the Ebola outbreak be stopped?

Yes. Experts know how to control Ebola. They are now working to stop the outbreak in West Africa, which is the best way to protect people in the U.S. and around the world. Once Ebola is brought under control in the infected countries,

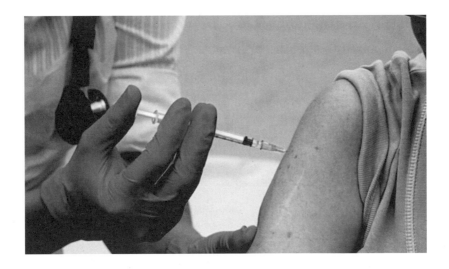

there will be no new cases and the virus will stop spreading. However, experts are unsure of how long it will take to end the current Ebola outbreak.

How is the U.S. helping?

Disease specialists have been sent to West Africa by the Centers for Disease Control and Prevention (CDC) to help slow the spread of Ebola.

READING COMPREHENSION

■ Indicate if each statement is true (T) or false (F) according to the reading.

1. _____ Ebola was given name from the Ebola Bridge in the Democratic Republic of Congo. The disease was first reported in a village on the bridge in 1972.

2. _____ Ebola is brought under control in the infected countries by USFWS.

3. _____ Ebola is not highly contagious.

4. _____ Ebola can be prevented spread.

5. _____ Since Dec. 2013, nearly 20,000 people have become infected with the Ebola virus, and more than 10,000 have died from it.

■ Discuss the following questions with your classmates.

1. Can you recognize Ebola virus? Is it fatal?

2. Have you come across the fact that even North Korea take strong action against Ebola?

3. Where is the origin of Ebola?

4. What is the role of the Centers for Disease Control and Prevention (CDC)?

5. Were there Ebola patients in S. Korea?

10 African Lions in Trouble

Experts want African lions to be listed as "threatened" under the Endangered Species Act

by Rishi Iyengar

The world's most iconic cat is in trouble. On Monday, the U.S. Fish and Wildlife Service (USFWS) asked for African lions to be listed as "threatened" under the Endangered Species Act. This move would help protect them from extinction.

The African lion population, in 1980, was predicted to be 75,800, according to the International Union for Conservation of Nature (IUCN). That number has dropped by 30%. The Fish and Wildlife Service adds that about 70% of all lion populations inhabit just 10 areas in eastern and southern Africa.

"Unless things improve, lions will face extinction," said Daniel Ashe, the director of the U.S. Fish and Wildlife Service.

Homes at Risk

A statement from the U.S. Fish and Wildlife Service listed the main threats to the big cats as loss of habitat, lack of prey, and more conflicts with humans. Over time, more humans have moved into areas inhabited by lions. Experts believe human population in sub-Saharan Africa will double by 2050, making the problem worse.

How the Title Would Help

By listing the species as endangered, the USFWS said it could help lions. The service could make some activities illegal, including the buying and selling of hunted lions as trophies. This, it said, would ensure "that people in the United States do not contribute to the further decline of listed species."

Fish and Wildlife Service director Daniel Ashe said the agency wants to protect the endangered animals as much as possible.

"It is up to all of us, not just the people of Africa, to ensure that healthy, wild populations continue to roam the savannah for generations to come," he said.

Wildlife expert Jane Goodall called the suggested listing "excellent news." She says people were not aware of the decline because they see the animals in parks.

"I hope that the proposed listing will be approved," Goodall told the *Washington Post*. "How terrible to lose the 'king of beasts' from the African scene."

READING COMPREHENSION

■ Indicate if each statement is true (T) or false (F) according to the reading.

1. _____ In this essay, the writer assures that African lions don't need the title, "endangered species."

2. _____ The number of African lions increased by 30%.

3. _____ The main threats to the lions are more conflicts with habitats.

4. _____ There are lots of lions in the Zoo but it doesn't mean the number of lions increased.

■ Discuss the following questions with your classmates.

1. What does USFWS stand for? Have you heard about it?

2. What is your opinion on endangered species?

3. How do you compare African lions with Korean lions?

4. How do you prevent the decreased number of African lions?

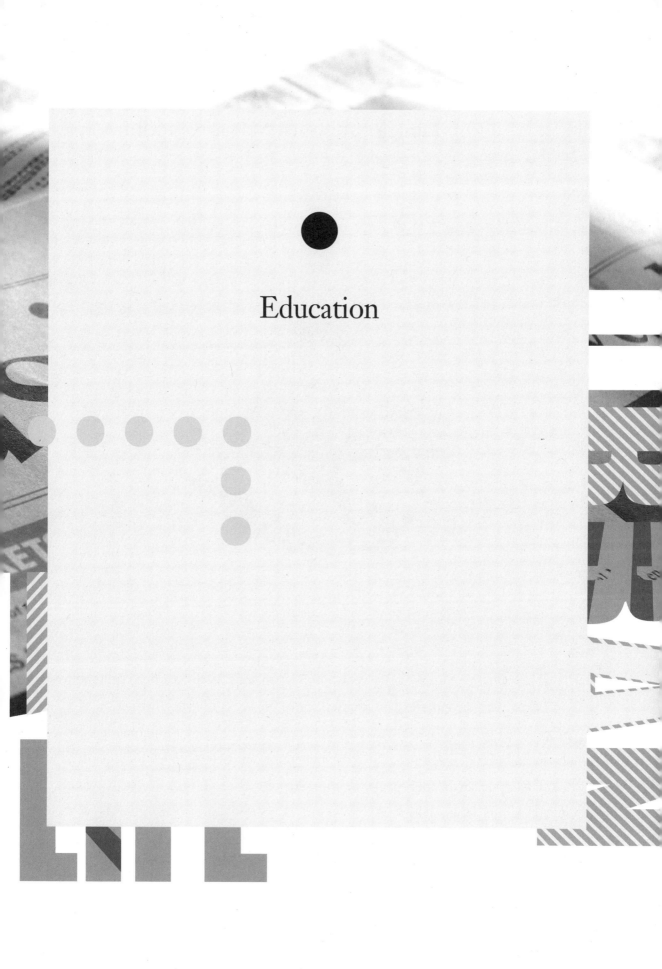

Education

11   The Development of Self in Childhood

by Kelvin L. Seifert et al.

How do we acquire a sense of identity, or self? Well, it doesn't happen overnight. In Europe and the United States, at least, identity formation is a process that involves several different steps, each occurring at a different age. By the second year of life, for example, most children can correctly label their gender, a key component in identity formation. Around two, children start to make statements like "I am a boy" or "I am a girl." Labels like these then pave the way for a later, more complete and more sophisticated sense of identity.

Initially, however, such labels lack permanence. Between the ages of two and three, a boy may claim he can become a girl under certain circumstances—"when I grow up" or "if I grow my hair long." Similarly, a girl might imagine she can change her gender by changing her name—"I'm going to call myself Bob and become a boy." At this early stage in identity formation, children are also prone to thinking they can throw off human identity and become an animal: "Bow-wow, I'm a dog."

After the age of five or six, however, children begin to develop a sense of self-constancy (the belief that identity remains permanently fixed). At this point, children start to believe that they will stay the same person indefinitely on into the future. They now believe that they will remain human forever and maintain the same gender under all circumstances. Permanent beliefs like these are the most basic and earliest core of a personal identity.

Around the age of eight, children begin to include psychological characteristics in their description of self. They say, for example, "I am brave" or "I am happy." What's missing from this early description of self is any sense of context. The child does not realize that he or she is brave in certain situations and fearful in others. Nor does the child recognize that he or she can be brave and fearful at the same time. Rather, the tendency is to focus on one particular feeling or trait and disregard all others. At this point, ambiguous, or conflicting, feelings seem too threatening to be expressed or even acknowledged, perhaps because the child's internal sense of identity still feels weak and fragile.

By the end of middle childhood, both boys and girls are clearly able to think of themselves in more complicated ways. They can, for example, describe themselves as relaxed and skillful when in the classroom but ill-at-ease or uncomfortable in social settings. They are now much less likely to define themselves in simplistic terms, i.e., "I am always angry." Instead, they are more likely to describe themselves in relation to particular situations: "I get angry when

I think people are not listening to what I have to say." But generally speaking, it isn't until adulthood that children develop a more flexible sense of self and are able to integrate, or combine, conflicting traits: "I am a friendly person and like to be around people, but I also need some time alone on a regular basis."

It's worth pointing out, however, that the process of creating and maintaining a sense of identity does not appear to be the same in all cultures. In Asian countries like India, Japan, and Nepal, for example, three distinct senses of self appear to develop in childhood and persist on into adulthood—the familial, the spiritual, and the individual. The familial self relates only to how one appears or behaves within the context of the family: "I am very obedient to my parents' wishes." In contrast, the spiritual self is defined and organized strictly in terms of religious beliefs: "My relationship to my god is central to my life." As one might expect, the individual self is closest to the European sense of identity described in the preceding paragraphs: "I am a generally happy person."

READING COMPREHENSION

■ Indicate if each statement is true (T) or false (F) according to the reading.

1. _____ In Europe and the United States, most 2-year-olds are able to label their gender.

2. _____ Between the ages of three and four, children tend to think that they can become an animal.

3. _____ Self-constancy is the belief that identity remains permanently fixed.

4. _____ Around the age of eight, the children's internal sense of identity is strong enough to express their feelings.

5. _____ In Asian countries, children appear to have three distinct senses of self like the familial, the spiritual and the individual.

■ Discuss the following questions with your classmates.

1. This essay deals with the development of self in childhood. According to age, children undergo the process of identity formation. Can you describe the process in which children's identities are shaped in order of age?

2. Children in Asian countries are different from those in European countries in that they create and maintain three senses of self, that is, the familial, the spiritual, and the individual. Do you agree with this reading passage?

3. It is said that your sense of identity gives you a sense of who you are as a person. What about you? If you want to know your identity, you have to understand both how you differ from others and how you are similar. Think about your personal identity.

12   The History of the Internet

by Casey Malarcher, Andrea Janzen, Adam Worcester

Almost everyone knows about the Internet. More than a billion people around the world are now online. The Internet is a powerful tool for information and communication.

The basic concept of the Internet was first thought of in the early 1960s. It began as a military research network, designed to be decentralized or spread out over many locations. If one location was attacked, the military could communicate from another location. The first small network went online in 1969. It connected four universities in the United States.

This network was very successful from the beginning. Scientists could now share information about their research. In 1972, email was invented and quickly became the most popular application. By the end of that year, the network connected many universities and government research centers. The general public became aware of the network in the late 70s. A new version allowed anyone to get online. People from all over the world joined online groups to talk about thousands of different subjects.

The term Internet was used for the first time in 1982. New technology had created a common language for the network computers. The Internet was now recognized as an international network. This was also at the time when privacy and security started becoming important issues. Hackers and viruses began to emerge.

In 1990, the original military network went offline, and a year later the World Wide Web was born. The World Wide Web is a global information network that allows users to access and navigate within information on the Internet. With the introduction of the World Wide Web, the development of the Internet accelerated at a rapid pace. The first computer code of the web was created in 1991 allowing programmers to combine words, pictures, and sounds on web pages.

In the early nineties, the first search engine, Gopher, and the first web browser, Mosaic, were developed, allowing easier and simpler access to the Net. Traffic on the Internet started growing at an annual rate of approximately 340,000 percent.

At the end of the 1990s, Internet2 was born. Internet2 uses fiber optic cables to link together a consortium of hundreds of high-speed networks around the world. Instead of connecting to the Internet solely through telephone lines, people could now connect in a wide variety of ways, including via satellite. These

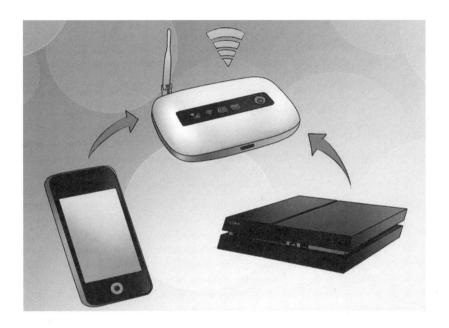

new methods have more data carrying capacity, or bandwidth, than telephone lines. This made the Internet faster and able to convey much more information. People could soon watch TV shows and movies online.

In the future, people will not need a computer to access the Internet. The browser will become a platform for the Web. Information will no longer need to be stored in a computer hard drive. Instead, it will be stored in places around the world. People can retrieve it through cell phones, music players, and other portable devices. This is called "cloud computing," because it seems as if information floats down from the sky. A 2008 study said that the Internet will continue to grow. By 2020, a low-cost global network will allow people even in remote areas to have Internet access. English will remain the primary Net language, but other languages, especially Mandarin, will increase. Also, a segment of society will refuse to use the Net and live without modern technology.

READING COMPREHENSION

■ Indicate if each statement is true (T) or false (F) according to the reading.

1. _____ The first small network had a bad influence on young people.

2. _____ The World Wide Web is a global information network that allows anyone to get online.

3. _____ The concept of the Internet came from academic research in the 1960s.

4. _____ People started to gain acquaintance with the network in the late 70s.

5. _____ By 2020, a low-priced global network will provide people in isolated areas with Internet access.

■ Discuss the following questions with your classmates.

1. How many portable devices do you have? Do you use your computer or cell phone to get online?

2. For what purpose do you usually access the Internet?

3. Can you imagine your life without the Internet?

People & Opinions

13 Three Ways of Responding to Oppression

by Martin Luther King, Jr.

Oppressed people deal with their oppression in three characteristic ways. One way is acquiescence: the oppressed resign themselves to their doom. They tacitly adjust themselves to oppression, and thereby become conditioned to it. In every movement toward freedom some of the oppressed prefer to remain oppressed. Almost 2800 years ago Moses set out to lead the children of Israel from the slavery of Egypt to the freedom of the promised land. He soon discovered that slaves do not always welcome their deliverers. They become accustomed to being slaves. They would rather bear those ills they have, as Shakespeare pointed out, than flee to others that they know not of. They prefer the "fleshpots of Egypt" to the ordeals of emancipation.

There is such a thing as the freedom of exhaustion. Some people are so worn down by the yoke of oppression that they give up. A few years ago in the slum areas of Atlanta, a Negro guitarist used to sing almost daily: "Ben down so long that down don't bother me." This is the type of negative freedom and resignation that often engulfs the life of the oppressed.

But this is not the way out. To accept passively an unjust system is to cooperate with that system; thereby the oppressed become as evil as the oppressor. Noncooperation with evil is as much a moral obligation as is cooperation with good. The oppressed must never allow the conscience of the oppressor to slumber. Religion reminds every man that he is his brother's keeper. To accept injustice or segregation passively is to say to the oppressor that his actions are morally right. It is a way of allowing his conscience to fall asleep. At this moment the oppressed fails to be his brother's keeper. So acquiescence—while often the easier way—is not the moral way. It is the way of the coward. The Negro cannot win the respect of his oppressor by acquiescing; he merely increases the oppressor's arrogance and contempt. Acquiescence is interpreted as proof of the Negro's inferiority. The Negro cannot win the respect of the white people of the South or the peoples of the world if he is willing to sell the future of his children for his personal and immediate comfort and safety.

A second way that oppressed people sometimes deal with oppression is to resort to physical violence and corroding hatred. Violence often brings about momentary results. Nations have frequently won their independence in battle. But in spite of temporary victories, violence never brings permanent peace. It solves no social problem; it merely creates new and more complicated ones.

Violence as a way of achieving racial justice is both impractical and immoral. It is impractical because it is a descending spiral ending in destruction for all. The old law of an eye for an eye leaves everybody blind. It is immoral because it seeks to humiliate the opponent rather than win his understanding; it seeks to annihilate rather than to convert. Violence is immoral because it thrives on hatred rather than love. It destroys community and makes brotherhood impossible. It leaves society in monologue rather than dialogue. Violence ends by defeating itself. It creates bitterness in the survivors and brutality in the destroyers. A voice echoes through time saying to every potential Peter, "Put up your sword." History is cluttered with the wreckage of nations that failed to follow this command.

If the American Negro and other victims of oppression succumb to the temptation of using violence in the struggle for freedom, future generations will be the recipients of a desolate night of bitterness, and our chief legacy to them will be an endless reign of meaningless chaos. Violence is not the way.

The third way open to oppressed people in their quest for freedom is the way of nonviolent resistance. Like the synthesis in Hegelian philosophy, the principle of nonviolent resistance seeks to reconcile the truths of two opposites—acquiescence and violence—while avoiding the extremes and immoralities of both. The nonviolent resister agrees with the person who acquiesces that one should not be physically aggressive toward his opponent; but he balances the equation by agreeing with the person of violence that evil must be resisted. He avoids the nonresistance of the former and the violent resistance of the latter. With nonviolent resistance, no individual or group need submit to any wrong, nor need anyone resort to violence in order to right a wrong.

It seems to me that this is the method that must guide the actions of the Negro in the present crisis in race relations. Through nonviolent resistance the Negro will be able to rise to the noble height of opposing the unjust system while

loving the perpetrators of the system. The Negro must work passionately and unrelentingly for full stature as a citizen, but he must not use inferior methods to gain it. He must never come to terms with falsehood, malice, hate, or destruction.

Nonviolent resistance makes it possible for the Negro to remain in the South and struggle for his rights. The Negro's problem will not be solved by running away. He cannot listen to the glib suggestion of those who would urge him to migrate en masse to other sections of the country. By grasping his great opportunity in the South he can make a lasting contribution to the moral strength of the nation and set a sublime example of courage for generations yet unborn.

By nonviolent resistance, the Negro can also enlist all men of good will in his struggle for equality. The problem is not a purely racial one, with Negroes set against whites. In the end, it is not a struggle between people at all, but a tension between justice and injustice. Nonviolent resistance is not aimed against oppressors but against oppression. Under its banner consciences, not racial groups, are enlisted.

If the Negro is to achieve the goal of integration, he must organize himself into a militant and nonviolent mass movement. All three elements are indispensable. The movement for equality and justice can only be a success if it has both a mass and militant character; the barriers to be overcome require both. Nonviolence is an imperative in order to bring about ultimate community.

A mass movement of a militant quality that is not at the same time committed to nonviolence tends to generate conflict, which in turn breeds anarchy. The support of the participants and the sympathy of the uncommitted are both inhibited by the threat that bloodshed will engulf the community. This reaction in turn encourages the opposition to threaten and resort to force. When, however, the mass movement repudiates violence while moving resolutely toward its goal, its opponents are revealed as the instigators and practitioners of violence if it occurs. Then public support is magnetically attracted to the advocates of nonviolence, while those who employ violence are literally disarmed by overwhelming sentiment against their stand.

READING COMPREHENSION

■ Indicate if each statement is true (T) or false (F) according to the reading.

1. _____ King asserts that acquiescence is construed as proof of the Negro's inferiority.

2. _____ King recommends that the oppressed choose violence as a way of achieving racial justice.

3. _____ King's civil rights movement caused a racial struggle between whites and blacks in America.

4. _____ According to King, nonviolent resistance is the best method that the oppressed must adopt to pursue their freedom.

5. _____ The Negro, King says, must organize himself into a militant and nonviolent mass movement for the goal of integration.

■ Discuss the following questions with your classmates.

1. What are the three ways of responding to oppression according to Martin Luther King? Define the three ways in your own words.

2. According to Martin Luther King, what is the best way for the oppressed people in their quest for freedom? Do you agree with him? Why or why not?

3. How much racism is there in your country?
   Discuss the forms of racism that exist in your country.

4. How much do you know about the civil rights movement?
   Talk about the history of the civil rights movement in your country as well as in the United States.

14 Steve Jobs' 2005 Stanford Commencement Address

by Steve Jobs

Thank you. I'm honored to be with you today for your commencement from one of the finest universities in the world. Truth be told, I never graduated from college and this is the closest I've ever gotten to a college graduation.

Today I want to tell you three stories from my life. That's it. No big deal. Just three stories. The first story is about connecting the dots.

I dropped out of Reed College after the first six months but then stayed around as a drop-in for another eighteen months or so before I really quit. So why did I drop out? It started before I was born. My biological mother was a young, unwed graduate student, and she decided to put me up for adoption. She felt very strongly that I should be adopted by college graduates, so everything was all set for me to be adopted at birth by a lawyer and his wife, except that when I popped out, they decided at the last minute that they really wanted a girl. So my parents, who were on a waiting list, got a call in the middle of the night asking, "We've got an unexpected baby boy. Do you want him?" They said, "Of course." My biological mother found out later that my mother had never graduated from college and that my father had never graduated from high school. She refused to sign the final adoption papers. She only relented a few months later when my parents promised that I would go to college.

This was the start in my life. And seventeen years later, I did go to college, but I naively chose a college that was almost as expensive as Stanford, and all of my working-class parents' savings were being spent on my college tuition. After six months, I couldn't see the value in it. I had no idea what I wanted to do with my life, and no idea of how college was going to help me figure it out, and here I was, spending all the money my parents had saved their entire life. So I decided to drop out and trust that it would all work out OK. It was pretty scary at the time, but looking back, it was one of the best decisions I ever made. The minute I dropped out, I could stop taking the required classes that didn't interest me and begin dropping in on the ones that looked far more interesting.

It wasn't all romantic. I didn't have a dorm room, so I slept on the floor in friends' rooms. I returned Coke bottles for the five-cent deposits to buy food with, and I would walk the seven miles across town every Sunday night to get one good meal a week at the Hare Krishna temple. I loved it. And much of what I stumbled into by following my curiosity and intuition turned out to be priceless later on. Let me give you one example.

Reed College at that time offered perhaps the best calligraphy instruction in the country. Throughout the campus every poster, every label on every drawer was beautifully hand-calligraphed. Because I had dropped out and didn't have to take the normal classes, I decided to take a calligraphy class to learn how to do this. I learned about serif and sans-serif typefaces, about varying the amount of space between different letter combinations, about what makes great typography great. It was beautiful, historical, artistically subtle in a way that science can't capture, and I found it fascinating.

None of this had even a hope of any practical application in my life. But ten years later when we were designing the first Macintosh computer, it all came back to me, and we designed it all into the Mac. It was the first computer with beautiful typography. If I had never dropped in on that single course in college, the Mac would have never had multiple typefaces or proportionally spaced fonts, and since Windows just copied the Mac, it's likely that no personal computer would have them.

If I had never dropped out, I would have never dropped in on that calligraphy class and personals computers might not have the wonderful typography that they do.

Of course it was impossible to connect the dots looking forward when I was in college, but it was very, very clear looking backwards 10 years later. Again, you can't connect the dots looking forward. You can only connect them looking backwards, so you have to trust that the dots will somehow connect in your future. You have to trust in something—your gut, destiny, life, karma, whatever—because believing that the dots will connect down the road will give you the confidence to follow your heart, even when it leads you off the well-worn path, and that will make all the difference.

My second story is about love and loss. I was lucky. I found what I loved to do early in life. Woz and I started Apple in my parents' garage when I was twenty. We worked hard and in ten years, Apple had grown from just the two of us in a garage into a $2 billion company with over 4,000 employees. We'd just released our finest creation, the Macintosh, a year earlier, and I'd just turned thirty, and then I got fired. How can you get fired from a company you started? Well, as Apple grew, we hired someone who I thought was very talented to run the company with me, and for the first year or so, things went well. But then our visions of the future began to diverge, and eventually we had a falling out. When we did, our board of directors sided with him, and so at thirty, I was out, and very publicly out. What had been the focus of my entire adult life was gone I, and it was devastating. I really didn't know what to do for a few months. I felt that I had let the previous generation of entrepreneurs down, that I had dropped the baton as it was being passed to me. I met with David Packard and Bob Noyce and tried to apologize for screwing up so badly. I was a very public failure and I even thought about running away from the Valley. But something slowly began to dawn on me. I still loved what I did. The turn of events at Apple had not changed that one bit. I'd been rejected but I was still in love. And so I decided to start over.

I didn't see it then, but it turned out that getting fired from Apple was the best thing that could have ever happened to me. The heaviness of being successful was replaced by the lightness of being a beginner again, less sure about everything. It freed me to enter one of the most creative periods in my life. During the next five years I started a company named NeXT, another company named Pixar and fell in love with an amazing woman who would become my wife. Pixar went on to create the world's first computer-animated feature film, "Toy Story," and is now the most successful animation studio in the world.

In a remarkable turn of events, Apple bought NeXT and I returned to Apple and the technology we developed at NeXT is at the heart of Apple's current renaissance, and Lorene and I have a wonderful family together.

I'm pretty sure none of this would have happened if I hadn't been fired from Apple. It was awful-tasting medicine but I guess the patient needed it. Sometimes life's going to hit you in the head with a brick. Don't lose faith. I'm convinced that the only thing that kept me going was that I loved what I did. You've got to find what you love, and that is as true for work as it is for your lovers. Your work is going to fill a large part of your life, and the only way to be truly satisfied is to do what you believe is great work, and the only to do great work is to do what you do. If you haven't found it yet, keep looking, and don't settle. As with all matters of the heart, you'll know when you find it, and like any great relationship it just gets better and better as the years roll on. So keep looking. Don't settle.

My third story is about death. When I was 17, I read a quote that went something like "If you live each day as if it was your last, someday you'll most certainly be right." It made an impression on me, and since then, for the past 33 years, I have looked in the mirror every morning and asked myself, "If today were the last day of my life, would I want to do what I am about to do today?" And whenever the answer has been "no" for too many days in a row, I know I need to change something. Remembering that I'll be dead soon is the most important tool I've ever encountered to help me make the big choices in life, because almost everything—all external expectations, all pride, all fear of embarrassment or failure—these things just fall away in the face of death, leaving only what is truly important. Remembering that you are going to die is the best way I know to avoid the trap of thinking you have something to lose. You are already naked. There is no reason not to follow your heart.

About a year ago, I was diagnosed with cancer. I had a scan at 7:30 in the morning and it clearly showed a tumor on my pancreas. I didn't even know what a pancreas was. The doctors told me this was almost certainly a type of cancer that is incurable, and that I should expect to live no longer than three to six months. My doctor advised me to go home and get my affairs in order, which is doctors' code for "prepare to die." It means to try and tell your kids everything you thought you'd have the next ten years to tell them, in just a few months. It means

to make sure that everything is buttoned up so that it will be as easy as possible for your family. It means to say your goodbyes.

I lived with that diagnosis all day. Later that evening I had a biopsy where they stuck an endoscope down my throat, through my stomach into my intestines, put a needle into my pancreas and got a few cells from the tumor. I was sedated but my wife, who was there, told me that when they viewed the cells under a microscope, the doctor started crying, because it turned out to be a very rare form of pancreatic cancer that is curable with surgery. I had the surgery and, thankfully, I am fine now.

This was the closest I've been to facing death, and I hope it's the closest I get for a few more decades. Having lived through it, I can now say this to you with a bit more certainty than when death was a useful but purely intellectual concept. No one wants to die, even people who want to go to Heaven don't want to die to get there, and yet, death is the destination we all share. No one has ever escaped it. And that is as it should be, because death is very likely the single best invention of life. It's life's change agent; it clears out the old to make way for the new. Right now, the new is you. But someday, not too long from now, you will gradually become the old and be cleared away. Sorry to be so dramatic, but it's quite true. Your time is limited, so don't waste it living someone else's life. Don't be trapped by dogma, which is living with the results of other people's thinking. Don't let the noise of others' opinions drown out your own inner voice, and most important, have the courage to follow your heart and intuition. They somehow already know what you truly want to become. Everything else is secondary.

When I was young, there was an amazing publication called 'The Whole Earth Catalogue,' which was one of the bibles of my generation. It was created by a fellow named Stuart Brand not far from here in Menlo Park, and he brought it to life with his poetic touch. This was in the late sixties, before personal computers and desktop publishing, so it was all made with typewriters, scissors, and Polaroid cameras. It was sort of like Google in paperback from thirty-five years before Google came along. It was idealistic, overflowing with neat tools and great notions. Stuart and his team put out several issues of the Whole Earth Catalogue, and then when it had run its course, they put out a final issue. It was the mid-nineteen seventies and I was your age. On the back cover of their final issue was a photograph of an early morning country road, the kind you might find yourself hitchhiking on if you were so adventurous. Beneath it were the words, "Stay hungry, stay foolish." It was their farewell message as they signed off. "Stay hungry, stay foolish." And I have always wished that for myself, and now, as you graduate to begin anew, I wish that for you. Stay hungry, stay foolish.

Thank you all, very much.

READING COMPREHENSION

■ Indicate if each statement is true (T) or false (F) according to the reading.

1. _____ Steve Jobs dropped out of college when he was a sophomore.

2. _____ Steve Jobs biological mother was an old, poor and unwed

   graduate student.

3. _____ Steve Jobs biological mother didn't want to put him up for adoption.

4. _____ Steve Jobs was diagnosed with cancer.

■ Discuss the following questions with your classmates.

1. Do you think going to university is important? Why or why not?

2. Are there other ways to learn skills besides going to school?

   Can you name a few?

3. "Sometimes the right decision may be not doing what is expected but

   following your heart." Do you agree with thin idea? Why or why not?

4. Do you know any respectable CEO? Who is she or he?

   Talk about admirable traits for a respectable CEO.

15 In an Uptrend, Women Marrying Younger Men

by Moon Gwang-lip

For Huh You-kyung, a 31-year-old attorney at a large law firm in Seoul, having a husband one year her junior is no longer too embarrassing to speak about. Huh, who married in 2006, recalled that her in-laws initially were a bit hesitant about the pairing, as it was rare to see a woman with a younger man—called a "yeonsang-yeonha" couple—at the time.

But Huh said the overall climate has changed significantly in just the past few years, and some of her female colleagues have even recently married men a decade or more younger than them. "People are rarely surprised to find out that I am living with a man who is younger," Huh said. "We consider each other more like friends, something that might be unthinkable for traditionally patriarchal couples, and I like that." Huh is part of a larger trend sweeping across Korea and much of the developed world as the role of women in society evolves.

According to recent data released by Statistics Korea, the number of marriages involving women who are older than men hit a record high in 2009. Among the 236,677 marriages in Korea last year where each side tied the knot for the first time, 33,794 - or 14.3 percent - involved older women and younger men, the data show. That is the highest portion since Statistics Korea began tracking such data in 1990.

The portion of marriages where the man and woman were the same age also rose to a record high of 16.1 percent. By the same token, marriages where the man was older than the woman fell below 70 percent of the total for the first time ever, coming in at 69.6 percent. That's a far cry from 1990, when 82.2 percent of newlywed wives had older husbands.

The same trend is true for those who remarried last year. Among the 31,765 marriages in this group, 73.4 percent, or 29,202, involved men who were older than the women. That's roughly unchanged from a year earlier, when the level hit a record low.

Analysts said the increase in the number of yeonsang-yeonha couples stems from the rising economic and social status of women in Korea's traditionally male-dominant society. Confucian beliefs that permeated throughout society during the 500-year rule of the Joseon Dynasty taught that men alone are responsible for supporting families financially and that the role of women should be confined to childbearing and household chores.

Today, however, women are increasingly venturing out into the corporate world. The country's low birthrate also is behind the trend, as the overall number of young women is shrinking, making it more difficult for men to find a junior

partner. "The number of women being born each year has been decreasing over the years," said an official with Statistics Korea. The official said the growth of yeonsang-yeonha couples will be a long-term trend.

READING COMPREHENSION

■ Indicate if each statement is true (T) or false (F) according to the reading.

1. _____ The number of marriages involving women who are older than

men is increasing.

2. _____ The portion of marriages where the man and woman were the

same age is decreasing.

3. _____ The increase in the number of "yeonsang-yeonha" couples is a

result of the rising economic status of women.

4. _____ Throughout Joseon Dynasty men alone were responsible for

supporting families financially.

5. _____ There are more marriages with younger men these days.

■ Discuss the following questions with your classmates.

1. Have you ever dated younger men(for females) or elder women(for males)?

If you don't mind, could you tell us your memories with him and her?

2. Have you seen couples(youger men and elder women)? What do you think

about the couples? And what is good and bad points of the couples?

3. If you chose your partner, would you wanna go out with or get married to

a younger man or an elder woman?

4. What is the change from the past and now in marriage?

Why do you think there were less marriage in the past?

16 Appointment with Love

by Sulamith Ish-Kishor

Six minutes to six, said the great round clock over the information booth in Grand Central Station. The tall young Army lieutenant who had just come from the direction of the tracks lifted his sunburned face, and his eyes narrowed to note the exact time. His heart was pounding with a beat that shocked him because he could not control it. In six minutes, he would see the woman who had filled such a special place in his life for the past thirteen months, the woman he had never seen, yet whose written words had been with him and sustained him unfailingly.

He placed himself as close as he could to the information booth, just beyond the ring of people besieging the clerks.

Lieutenant Blandford remembered one night in particular, the worst of the fighting, when his place had been caught in the midst of a pack of Zeros. He had seen the grinning face of one of the Jap pilots.

In one of his letters, he had confessed to her that he often felt fear, and only a few days before this battle, he had received her answer: "Of course you fear... all brave men do. Didn't King David know fear? That's why he wrote the Twenty-third Psalm. Next time you doubt yourself, I want you to hear my voice reciting to you: 'Yea, though I walk in the valley of the shadow of death, I shall fear no evil, for Thou art with me'..." And he had remembered: he had heard her imagined voice, and it had renewed his strength and skill. Now he was going to hear her real voice. Four minutes to six. His face grew sharp.

Under the immense, starred roof, people were walking fast, like threads of color being woven into a gray web. A girl passed close to him, and lieutenant Blandford stared. She was wearing a red flower in her suit lapel, but it was a crimson sweet pea, not the little red rose they had agreed upon. Besides, this girl was too young; about eighteen, whereas Hollis Meynell had frankly told him she was thirty. "Well, what of it?" He had answered. "I'm thirty-two." He was twenty-nine.

His mind went back to that book—the book the Lord Himself must have put into his hands out of the hundreds of Army library books sent to the Florida training camp. *Of Human Bondage* it was; and throughout the book were notes in a woman's writing. He had always hated that writing-in habit, but these remarks were different. He had never believed that a woman could see into a man's heart so tenderly, so understandingly. Her name was on the bookplate: Hollis Meynell. He had got hold of a New York City telephone book and found her addresd. He had written, she had answered. Next day he had been shipped out, but they had went on writing. For thirteen months, she had faithfully replied, and more than replied. When his letters did not arrive, she wrote anyway, and now he believed he loved her, and she loved him. But she had refused all his pleas to send him her photograph. That seemed rather bad, of course. But she had explained: "If your feeling for me has any reality, any honest basis, what I look like won't matter. Suppose I'm beautiful. I'd always be haunted by the feeling that you had been taking a chance on just that, and that kind of love would disgust me. Suppose I'm plain (and you must admit that this is more likely), then I'd always fear that you were only going on writing to me because you were lonely and had no one else. No, don't ask for my picture. When you come to New York, you shall see me and then you shall make your decision. Remember, both of us are free to stop or to go on after that—whichever we choose…"

One minute to six… he pulled hard on a cigarette. Then lieutenant Blandford's heart leaped higher than his plane had ever done. A young woman was coming toward him. Her figure was long and slim; her blond hair lay one in curls from her delicate ears. Her eyes were blue as flowers, her lips and chin had a gentle firmness. In her pale green suit, she was like springtime come alive. He started toward her, entirely forgetting to notice that she was wearing no rose, and as he moved, a small, provocative smile curved her lips.

"Going my way, soldier?" she murmured.

Uncontrollably, he made one step closer to her. Then he saw Hollis Meynell. She was standing almost directly behind the girl, a woman well past forty, her graying hair tucked under a worn hat. She was more then plump; her thick-ankled feet were thrust into low-heeled shoes. But she wore a red rose in the rumpled lapel of her brown coat. The girl in the green suit was walking quickly away.

Blandford felt as though he were being split in two, so keen was his desire to follow the girl, yet so deep was his longing for the woman whose spirit had truly companioned and upheld his own; and there she stood. Her pale, plump face was

gentle and sensible; he could see that now. Her gray eyes had a warm, kindly twinkle.

Lieutenant Blandford did not hesitate. His fingers gripped the small, worn, blue leather copy of *Of Human Bondage*, which was to identify him to her. This would not be love, but it would be something precious, something perhaps even rarer than love–a friendship for which he had been and must ever be grateful.

He squared his broad shoulders, saluted and held the book out toward the woman, although even while he spoke he felt choked by the bitterness of his disappointment.

"I'm lieutenant John Blandford, and you—you are Miss Meynell. I'm so glad you could meet me. May—may I take you to dinner?"

The woman's face broadened in a tolerant smile. "I don't know what this is all about, son," she answered. "That young lady in the green suit, who just went by, she begged me to wear this rose on my coat. And she said that if you asked me to go out with you, I should tell you that she's waiting for you in that big restaurant across the street. She said it was some kind of a test. I've got two boys with Uncle Sam myself, so I didn't mind to oblige you."

READING COMPREHENSION

■ Indicate if each statement is true (T) or false (F) according to the reading.

1. _____ Blandford have met Miss Meynell in the past.

2. _____ Hollis Meynell sent her photo to Blanford.

3. _____ In the worst fight night, Blandford saw Miss Meynell.

4. _____ Blandford was supposed to wear little red rose on his lapel
   When they meet at the station.

5. _____ When Blandford and Miss Meynell meet at the Grand Central,
   They made a deal but to go out continuously together.

■ Discuss the following questions with your classmates.

1. Do you like this love story? Why or why not?

2. What is your favorite love story? Talk about it with your classmates.

3. What is true love and how do you know when you have found it?

4. Do you believe in true love? Why or why not?

17   Cell Phones: Hang up or Keep Talking?

by Linda Lee & Erik Gundersen

Millions of people are using cell phones today. In many places it is actually considered unusual not to use one. In many countries, cell phones are very popular with young people. They find that the phones are more than a means of communication—having a mobile phone shows that they are cool and connected.

The explosion around the world in mobile phone use has some health professionals worried. Some doctors are concerned that in the future many people may suffer health problems from the use of mobile phones. In England, there has

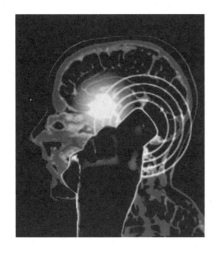

been a serious debate about this issue. Mobile phone companies are worried about the negative publicity of such ideas. They say that there is no proof that mobile phones are bad for your health.

On the other hand, why do some medical studies show changes in the brain cells of some people who use mobile phones? Signs of change in the tissues of the brain and head can be detected with modern scanning equipment. In one case, a traveling salesman had to retire at a young age because of serious memory loss. He couldn't remember even simple tasks. He would often forget the name of his own son. This man used to talk on his mobile phone for about six hours a day, every day of his working week, for a couple of years. His family doctor blamed his mobile phone use, but his employer's doctor didn't agree.

What is it that makes mobile phones potentially harmful? The answer is radiation. High-tech machines can detect very small amounts of radiation from mobile phones. Mobile phone companies agree that there is some radiation, but they say the amount is too small to worry about.

As the discussion about their safety continues, it appears that it's best to use mobile phones less often. Use your regular phone if you want to talk for a long time. Use your mobile phone only when you really need it. Mobile phones can be very useful and convenient, especially in emergencies. In the future, mobile phones may have a warning label that says they are bad for your health. So for now, it's wise not to use your mobile phone too often.

READING COMPREHENSION

■ Indicate if each statement is true (T) or false (F) according to the reading.

1. _____ It is wise to use your mobile phone these days.

2. _____ In the future people will suffer from diseases due to

   mobile phone use.

3. _____ The phones are not more than a means of communication.

4. _____ Some medical studies show changes in the brain cells of some

   people who use mobile phones.

■ Discuss the following questions with your classmates.

1. What are the advantages and disadvantages of cell phones?

   Compare mobile phones with regular phones?

2. Mobile phone companies agree that there is some radiation,

   but they say the amount is too small to worry about.

   Do you agree with them? Why or why not?

3. Talk about the possible dangers of cell phone use and the ways to avoid it.

4. Do you think cell phones should be allowed in school? Why or why not?

Aung San Suu Kyi's Silence on Burma's Human-Rights Abuses Is Appalling

by Charlie Campbell

The Nobel laureate's refusal to condemn documented atrocities suggests that political calculation has trumped human rights in her thinking.

Nobel laureate Aung San Suu Kyi is not happy with in Burma, officially now known as Myanmar. On Wednesday, the Nobel Peace Prize winner gave a press conference to denounce the "stalling" reform process.

"The U.S. government has been too optimistic," she said. "What significant reform steps have been taken in the last 24 months?"

This remark comes days before U.S. President Barack Obama's visit to Rangoon, and after talks to reform the nation's much maligned constitution broke down between Suu Kyi, Burma's powerful military generals, the current military-backed government and various ethnic leaders.

The constitution bars Suu Kyi from becoming President in next year's elections because she was married to a British man and has two sons who are foreign citizens. It also guarantees 25% of legislative seats to military appointees. Since more than 75% of lawmakers are required to enact any constitutional change, this gives the generals a de facto parliamentary veto.

Talks aimed at amending these provisions, which were shamelessly included with the sole purpose of barring Suu Kyi from the nation's highest office, have gone nowhere, and the 69-year-old is attempting one last throw of the dice appealing to Obama to put pressure on current President Thein Sein, himself a former junta general.

"Democratic reform would not be successful alone with the parliament," Suu Kyi told assembled media.

Nobody would argue against Burma's current constitution desperately needing revision, or pretend that reforms haven't stalled. In fact, when Obama returns to Burma next week, he will find one of his few foreign policy successes in tatters.

"The hope and the optimism we had in 2012, when the country was opening up, has all been squandered," Aung Zaw, managing editor of the Irrawaddy magazine, tells TIME, lamenting a "backsliding reform process" akin to watching "a train wreck in slow motion."

Even so, Suu Kyi's condemnation is curious.

It comes after her steadfast refusal to criticize the military or the government for myriad human-rights abuses. In Burma's west, for example, more than 100,000

Rohingya Muslims languish in squalid displacement camps, but Suu Kyi evidence-based of ethnic cleansing by Human Rights Watch and instead the crisis an "immigration issue."

In northernmost Kachin state, civilians face "attacks against civilian populations, extrajudicial killings, sexual violence, arbitrary arrest and detention, internal displacement, land confiscation, the recruitment of child soldiers, forced labor and portering." That's been by the U.N., but Suu Kyi has refused to condemn those atrocities. Her silence is so pointed that 23 local NGOs signed an open letter of protest.

Other causes of concern, like the 10 journalists this year on the flimsiest of pretenses, are brushed aside with platitudinous references to the "rule of law." Meanwhile, Suu Kyi's own Rule of Law Parliamentary Committee has achieved "nothing at all," says Aung Zaw.

"We would've liked to have seen Aung San Suu Kyi speak on human-rights issues in a more forthright way," says Matthew Smith, executive director of the Fortify Rights advocacy group. "She's issued equivocal statements on serious human-rights violations, in some cases amounting to crimes against humanity."

In fact, when a high-level delegation from Human Rights Watch came to Burma earlier this year for landmark talks, they met with senior government officials including the President but were snubbed by Suu Kyi.

And that's not all. Suu Kyi's baffling behavior goes beyond the area of human rights.

In April 2013, peaceful protesters blockaded a Chinese-owned copper mine near Monywa, around 450 miles north of Rangoon. The police using white phosphorous, leaving dozens with horrific burns, including traditionally sacrosanct Buddhist monks.

Suu Kyi headed the investigation commission but found that the mine must continue operations or else risk "hurting Burma," despite the fact that it is

desecrating the environment, was set up without scrutiny by the junta, and provides no jobs for local people. In unprecedented scenes, the National League for Democracy (NLD) leader was by furious locals.

Suu Kyi has certainly experienced enormous personal sacrifice. Since returning to her homeland in 1988, she has spent 15 years under house arrest, not even being able to see her beloved husband Michael Aris before he died.

But this is also why her current aloofness is so painful to behold.

"The NLD under her leadership has had big question marks," says Aung Zaw, "and they misread the whole situation."

In August 2011, Suu Kyi met Thein Sein for the first time, formally marking her belated return to mainstream politics. The following April, she and 42 NLD colleagues were elected to parliament in a landslide amid jubilant scenes.

The common perception among analysts is that some deal was struck to allow Suu Kyi to stand for election in exchange for muting her criticism of the generals. The presumption was that reforms would take baby steps forward. But, three years on, there has been no progress, and she is partly culpable.

When Suu Kyi finally gave her Nobel acceptance speech in June 2012 the prize having been originally bestowed in 1991 during a period of house arrest, she said that "receiving the Nobel Peace Prize means personally extending my concerns for democracy and human rights beyond national borders."

But her present recalcitrance suggests that her own political career may be more important, even if we accept the mitigation that it is for some vague greater good.

"There is no version of pragmatism that would make silence on human-rights atrocities defensible," says Smith. "These are some of the most serious human-rights violations that can be committed."

Admittedly, Suu Kyi has always said she is a politician, rather than a human-rights defender. But the truth today is that she is pretty awful at both.

READING COMPREHENSION

■ Indicate if each statement is true (T) or false (F) according to the reading.

1. _____ Suu Kyi rejected her Nobel acceptance speech in June 2012.

2. _____ The constitution allows Suu Kyi from becoming President in next year's elections because she was married to a British man and has two sons who are foreign citizens.

3. _____ Suu Kyi has always she is a politician, rather than a human-rights defender.

■ Discuss the following questions with your classmates.

1. Do you recognize Aung San Suu Kyi?

2. Working with your partner, make a timeline of Aung San Suu Kyi's life include many things as you can.

3. What impact do you think Aung San Suu Kyi's religious beliefs have had on her life?

4. Do you think she should have won Nobel Peace Prize? Why?

5. Why Suu Kyi is not welcomed by her country?

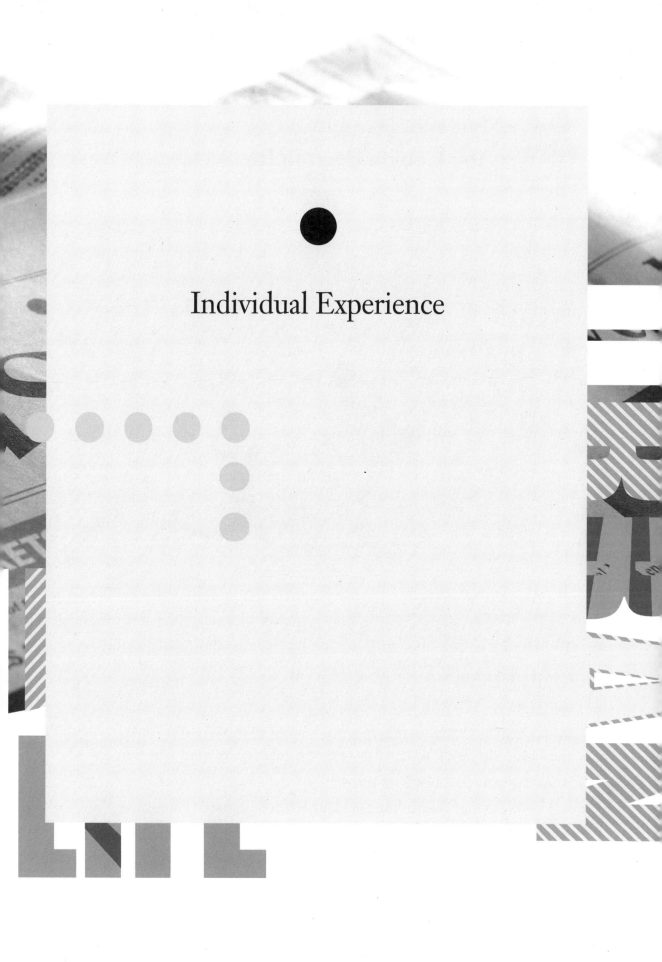

Individual Experience

19 Fun, Oh Boy. Fun. You Could Die from It

by Suzanne Britt Jordan

Fun is hard to have.

Fun is a rare jewel.

Somewhere along the line people got the modern idea that fun was there for the asking, that people deserved fun, that if we didn't have a little fun every day we would turn into (sakes alive!) puritans.

"Was it fun?" became the question that overshadowed all other questions: good questions like: Was it moral? Was it kind? Was it honest? Was it beneficial?

Was it generous? Was it necessary? And (my favorite) was it selfless?

When the pleasure got to be the main thing, the fun fetish was sure to follow. Everything was supposed to be fun. If it wasn't fun, then by Jove, we were going to make it fun, or else.

Think of all the things that got the reputation of being fun. Family outings were supposed to be fun. Sex was supposed to be fun. Education was supposed to be fun. Work was supposed to be fun. Walt Disney was supposed to be fun. Church was supposed to be fun. Staying fit was supposed to be fun.

Just to make sure that everybody knew how much fun we were having, we put happy faces on flunking test papers, dirty bumpers, sticky refrigerator doors, bathroom mirrors.

If a kid, looking at his very happy parents traipsing through that very happy Disney World, said, "This ain't fun, ma," his ma's heart sank. She wondered where she had gone wrong. Everybody told her what fun family outings to Disney World would be. Golly gee, what was the matter?

Fun got to be such a big thing that everybody started to look for more and more thrilling ways to supply it. One way was to step up the level of danger or licentiousness or alcohol or drug consumption so that you could be sure that, no matter what, you would manage to have a little fun.

Television commercials brought a lot of fun and fun-loving folks into the picture. Everything that people in those commercials did looked like fun: taking Polaroid snapshots, swilling beer, buying insurance, mopping the floor, bowling, or taking aspirin. We all wished, I'm sure, that we could have half as much fun as those rough-and-ready guys around the locker room, flicking each other with towels and pouring champagne. The more commercials people watched, the more they wondered when the fun would start in their own lives. It was pretty depressing.

Big occasions were supposed to be fun. Christmas, Thanksgiving and Easter

were obviously supposed to be fun. Your wedding day was supposed to be fun. Your wedding night was supposed to be a whole lot of fun. Your honeymoon was supposed to be the epitome of fundom. And so we ended up going through every Big Event we ever celebrated, waiting for the fun to start.

It occurred to me, while I was sitting around waiting for the fun to start, that not much is, and that I should tell you just in case you're worried about your fun capacity.

I don't mean to put a damper on things. I just mean we ought to treat fun reverently. It is a mystery. It cannot be caught like a virus. It cannot be trapped like an animal. The god of mirth is paying us back for all those years of thinking fun was everywhere by refusing to come to our party. I don't want to blaspheme fun anymore. When fun comes in on little dancing feet, you probably won't be expecting it. In fact, I bet it comes when you're doing your duty, your job, or your work. It may even come on a Tuesday.

I remember one day, long ago, on which I had an especially good time. Pam Davis and I walked to the College Village drug store one Saturday morning to buy some candy. We were about 12 years old (fun ages). She got her Bit-O-Honey. I got my malted milk balls, chocolate stars, Chunkys, and a small bag of M & M's. We started back to her house. I was going to spend the night. We had the whole day to look forward to. We had plenty of candy. It was a long way to Pam's house but every time we got weary Pam would put her hand over her eyes, scan the horizon like a sailor and say, "Oughta reach home by nightfall," at which point the two of us would laugh until we thought we couldn't stand it another minute. Then after we got calm, she'd say it again. You should have been there. It was the kind of day and friendship and occasion that made me deeply regretful that I had to grow up.

It was fun.

READING COMPREHENSION

■ Indicate if each statement is true (T) or false (F) according to the reading.

1. _____ Jordan defines that fun is easy to have.

2. _____ Jordan says that everybody thinks the family outings to
   Disney World were supposed to be fun.

3. _____ Jordan describes that modern people got to think that fun was
   there for the asking, that people deserved fun.

4. _____ According to Jordan, people have a secret desire to pursue
   pleasure to escape from the boredom of their everyday life.

5. _____ Jordan suggests that people should treat fun not blasphemously,
   but reverently.

■ Discuss the following questions with your classmates.

1. What are some of the ways Jordan says people make fun even more thrilling?

2. We find ourselves having more fun on TV commercials in which funny-looking
   and fun-loving folks appear. What do you think are the advantages
   and disadvantages of watching funny TV commercials.

3. Discuss the relationship between big occasions and the experience of fun.
   Have you ever tried to have more fun in your life?

20 Truly Alive

by James Collins

A jump turn and through Gate B I entered a new world. It was a world of exhilaration; a world of beauty, of love, of hope and of serenity. "Watch out for that boulder!" "Tree on your left!" "Follow that line!" were such simple survival commands we uttered as explorers of this terra incognita. Blood rushed, spirits flew, and minds soared. The world we once knew was a distant memory, a long-forgotten thing of the past. The mere three and a half hours spent in our paradise fills me with a lifetime of stirring memories.

It was Killebrew Canyon on the Nevada side of Lake Tahoe's Heavenly Mountain. Of the two canyons, Killebrew is certainly the road less traveled. Warning signs are posted everywhere alerting skiers and boarders to the treacherous trek back to the Mott Canyon lift (the only way home). Killebrew is a desolate and hidden area. Protected by its entrance gates and warning signs and lying well off the beaten path, it is a well-kept secret. One place, one world, I never would have found had I not met two people I will never forget.

Riding up the Dipper Express, I couldn't help but ask my lift-mates if they had skied the Dipperknob Trees. The area looked interesting on the map and caught my eye. They hadn't been there. I was a bit disappointed, but I found easy conversation about the amazing if not perfect ski conditions. It had snowed over a foot the night before leaving a powdery white blanket across the land. I soon asked the two people, presumably a married couple, where they had been on the mountain. They spoke as if they had seen something unearthly. Their words, inviting to a skier's soul, left me no other choice than to follow them to Killebrew.

We skied across the mountain and glided into the woods where Gate B emerged into view. They warned me that the canyon would eat anything less than an expert skier. With a gulp, I accepted their challenge and quickly asked them about the long trek mentioned on the warning sign. They chuckled a bit, and I dared not ask any further questions. We then crossed into paradise. I gasped at the beauty. The pristine blue sky, the majestic trees, the foreboding cliffs, the perfectly white surface. It was the first time I had ever seen something of such ineffable beauty. The colors and dancing light were like transcendent chords of a musical masterpiece that had taken on visible form—euphoric tones transformed into snowdrifts, icicles, and evergreens. Everything collapsed into the simplicity that surrounded me. And suddenly they were skiing; I had to follow.

They flowed down the mountain with liquid precision in perfect harmony. We dodged trees, jumped cliffs, and navigated waist-high powder. It was true

adventure, as we fought and found our way down. Jump turns, knee bends, and pole plants kept us from being consumed by the mountain. And as we hit the bottom I too chuckled. There was no trek. It was a short and scenic trail right to the lift. Certainly, it is no mistake that Killebrew is kept a secret.

As the day warmed up, conversation flowed, and ski masks were removed. I found myself shocked that I had been skiing with a retired couple in their sixties. My respect for their skiing abilities slowly grew into admiration for who they were. They were kind and peaceful, wise and without pretense. As the last run of the day approached I decided to go off on my own and explore a few parts of Killebrew that we hadn't seen. I reached the bottom rather quickly and waited for my newfound friends. Five minutes passed and I wished that I was still skiing. But five minutes soon turned into half an hour, and I began to worry. Thoughts rushed through my head. I feared the mountain had claimed the two people I thought would live forever. But, as I was on my way to the Ski Patrol, I heard a noise in the woods. It was them!

I had to hold myself back from running up and hugging them. They had no clue how long they had been gone. They simply told me they took their time and thanked me for waiting for them. The ski day was over. I went one way, they the other. I never saw them again. Their memory fulfills my definitions of love, hope, beauty, and serenity. And now, whenever I see a perfect blue sky or perhaps feel a cool breeze, I am reminded of my friends and of that day when I was truly alive.

READING COMPREHENSION

■ Indicate if each statement is true (T) or false (F) according to the reading.

1. _____ Collins has a memorable experience of snowboarding at

   Killebrew Canyon.

2. _____ Killebrew Canyon is on the Nevada side of Lake Tahoe's

   Heavenly Mountain.

3. _____ Killebrew is a desolate and hidden area which is less traveled.

4. _____ Collins met two young people he will never forget as he was skiing.

5. _____ Collins was enraptured over the beauty of the surroundings

   at the Canyon.

■ Discuss the following questions with your classmates.

1. Have you ever gone skiing at the ski resort? What is your favorite sport?

   Do you like outdoor or indoor sports? Why?

2. When you exercise to keep in shape, how many hours do you do in a week?

   Do you prefer to exercise alone or together?

3. Do you have any unforgettable memories of the sports? What are they?

21 My Responsibility

by David J. Bright

When she hung up the phone, she immediately burst into tears and grabbed out in all directions for something to hold onto as she sank to the floor. I stood there motionless, not knowing what to do, not knowing what to say, not even knowing what had happened. It wasn't until I answered the door moments later and saw the police officers standing in the alcove that I finally discovered what had taken place. My fifteen-year-old brother had been arrested. It was only ten days before Christmas, a year ago today when it happened, but still I remember it like yesterday.

Robert had always been a rambunctious as a child—wild and lively, as my mom always said. He was constantly joking around, playing pranks, and causing mayhem, but his engaging personality and small stature always seemed to save him from the firing line. This gave him the notion that he could cause any amount of trouble without feeling the repercussions. As a youngster growing up in Ireland, he had found few opportunities to get into a great deal of trouble. But four years ago at the age of twelve, the rules changed for him when he, my mother and I moved to America.

The same short stature that had been his ally in Ireland was now Robert's enemy in America. He was bullied and beaten on a daily basis. Since I couldn't be there all the time, Robert sought the protection from others. By the end of his first year in America, he had already joined a gang.

His appearance deteriorated, personality disappeared, and aggressiveness increased, leaving him an angry, hollowed out, manic depressive. After a year or so, his frighteningly self-destructive behavior and terrifying appearance forced my mom to send him to a suicide treatment center. There he received round the clock attention, counseling, and medication for his depression and aggressiveness. He was released after a couple of months.

Only a few short weeks later, supposedly after mixing his medication with alcohol, he went out with his friends to go to the store. There they robbed, shot, and killed a store clerk. Robert, as an accomplice to the crime, was charged with armed robbery and second degree murder.

Looking back now, I realize not what Robert had done wrong, but what I had done wrong. I had taken no interest in his welfare, and I never intervened when he needed me to. I just sat back and let it all come crashing down around me. It's in this respect that I guess I've changed the most. I'm now a much more involved person. I no longer allow things to just happen; I must be a part of everything that

affects me. I'm also a more caring and better person. To make up for what I did—or rather, didn't do—I look out for those around me, my family and my friends. I act like a big brother to them to compensate for not being any kind of brother at all to Robert.

The experience hasn't only made me better. In a strange way, it was also the best thing that could have happened to Robert. He's turned his life around and is presently preparing to take the SATs in anticipation to go on to college, something the old Robert would never have done.

I guess it's sort of weird, isn't it. Such a dreadful experience can change an entire family's life, and how such a tragic situation could give birth to such great things.

READING COMPREHENSION

■ Indicate if each statement is true (T) or false (F) according to the reading.

1. _____ Robert, David's brother, was nineteen years old when he was arrested.

2. _____ Robert used to be a wild and lively boy who liked to joke around and create chaos.

3. _____ Bright realized that he had taken too much interest in his brother's welfare.

4. _____ Looking back now, Bright finds himself at fault and becomes mature enough to learn from his mistakes.

5. _____ Bright is now a much more involved person who decides to make up for what he didn't do for Robert.

■ Discuss the following questions with your classmates.

1. This essay portrays Bright and his brother Robert's personal development from their own mistakes. Describe how their lives changed after a negative experience.

2. What are the biggest mistakes you have ever made in your life? If you could correct one mistake in your life, what would it be?

3. Do you know anyone who changed his or her life after a dreadful experience? How did he or she deal with the mistakes?

22 Barack Obama's Keynote Address at the Democratic National Convention

by Barack Obama

Tonight is a particular honor for me because, let's face it, my presence on this stage is pretty unlikely. My father was a foreign student, born and raised in a small village in Kenya. He grew up herding goats, went to school in a tin-roof shack. His father, my grandfather, was a cook, a domestic servant to the British. But my grandfather had larger dreams for his son. Through hard work and perseverance my father got a scholarship to study in a magical place, America, that shone as a beacon of freedom and opportunity to so many who had come before him.

While studying here, my father met my mother. She was born in a town on the other side of the world, in Kansas. … My parents shared not only an improbable love; they shared an abiding faith in the possibilities of this nation. They would give me an African name, Barack, or "blessed," believing that in a tolerant America, your name is no barrier to success. They imagined me going to the best schools in the land, even though they weren't rich, because in a generous America you don't have to be rich to achieve your potential. …

Tonight, we gather to affirm the greatness of our nation not because of the height of our skyscrapers, or the power of our military, or the size of our economy; our pride is based on a very simple premise, summed up in a declaration made over two hundred years ago: "We hold these truths to be self-evident, that all men are created equal, that they are endowed by their Creator with certain inalienable rights, that among these are life, liberty and the pursuit of happiness."

That is the true genius of America, a faith in simple dreams, an insistence on small miracles; that we can tuck in our children at night and know that they are fed and clothed and safe from harm; that we can say what we think, write what we think, without hearing a sudden knock on the door; that we can have an idea and start our own business without paying a bribe; that we can participate in the political process without fear of retribution; and that our votes will be counted. …

And fellow Americans, I say to you, tonight, we have more work to do—more work to do for the workers I met in Galesburg, Illinois, who are losing their union jobs at the Maytag plant that's moving to Mexico, and now they're having to compete with their own children for jobs that pay seven bucks an hour; more to do for the father I met who was losing his job and choking back the tears, wondering how he would pay $4,500 a month for the drugs his son needs without the health benefits that he counted on; more to do for the young woman in East St. Louis, and thousands more like her who have the grades, have the drive, have the will, but don't have the money to go to college.

Now don't get me wrong. The people I meet—in small towns and big cities, in diners and office parks—they don't expect the government to solve all their problems. They know they have to work hard to get ahead and they want to. Go into the collar countries around Chicago, and people will tell you they don't want their tax money wasted, by a welfare agency or by the Pentagon. Go into any inner city neighborhood, and folks will tell you that government alone can't teach our kids to learn—they know that parents have to teach, that children can't achieve unless we raise their expectations and turn off the television sets and eradicate the slander that says a black youth with a book is acting white. They know those things.

People don't expect the government to solve all their problems. But they sense, deep in their bones, that with just a slight change in priorities, we can make sure that every child in America has a decent shot at life, and that the doors of opportunity remain open to all.

READING COMPREHENSION

■ Indicate if each statement is true (T) or false (F) according to the reading.

1. _____ Obama's father was born and raised in a small village in America.

2. _____ While Obama's father was studying in university,

    he met Obama's mother.

3. _____ Obama's parents thought that they have to be rich to achieve their

    goals in America.

4. _____ Obama believes that government programs should solve all

    social problems.

5. _____ According to Obama, America is a tolerant nation,

    where people are treated equally.

■ Discuss the following questions with your classmates.

1. America is known as the country of freedom and opportunity.

    Do you think so? Why or why not?

2. Do you think all people have the right to life, liberty,

    and the pursuit of happiness no matter who they are?

3. In what ways do you think people are given an unfair treatment in Korea?

    What can be done to solve the social problems?

23   What I've Learned from Men

by Barbara Ehrenreich

For many years I believed that women had only one thing to learn from men: how to get the attention of a waiter by some means short of kicking over the table and shrieking. Never in my life have I gotten the attention of a waiter, unless it was an off-duty waiter whose car I'd accidentally scraped in a parking lot somewhere. Men, however, can summon a maître d' just by thinking the word "coffee," and this is a power women would be well advised to study. What else would we possibly want to learn from them? How to interrupt someone in mid-sentence as if you were performing an act of conversational euthanasia? How to drop a pair of socks three feet from an open hamper and keep right on walking? How to make those weird guttural gargling sounds in the bathroom?

But now, at mid-life, I am willing to admit that there are some real and useful things to learn from men. Not from all men—in fact, we may have the most to learn from some of the men we like the least. This realization does not mean that my feminist principles have gone soft with age: what I think women could learn from men is how to get *tough*. After more than a decade of consciousness-raising, assertiveness training, and hand-to-hand combat in the battle of the sexes, we're still too ladylike. Let me try that again—we're just too *damn* ladylike.

Here is an example from my own experience, a story that I blush to recount. A few years ago, at an international conference held in an exotic and luxurious setting, a prestigious professor invited me to his room for what he said would be an intellectual discussion on matters of theoretical importance. So far, so good. I showed up promptly. But only minutes into the conversation—held in all-too-adjacent chairs—it emerged that he was interested in something more substantial than a meeting of minds. I was disgusted, but not enough to overcome 30-odd years of programming in ladylikeness. Every time his comments took a lecherous turn, I chattered distractingly; every time his hand found its way to my knee, I returned it as if it were something he had misplaced. This went on for an unconscionable period (as much as 20 minutes); then there was a minor scuffle, a dash for the door, and I was out—with nothing violated but my self-esteem. I, a full-grown feminist, conversant with such matters as rape crisis counselling and sexual harassment at the workplace, had behaved like a ninny—or, as I now understand it, like a lady.

The essence of ladylikeness is a persistent servility masked as "niceness." For example, we (women) tend to assume that it is our responsibility to keep everything "nice" even when the person we are with is rude or aggressive. (In the above example, I was so busy taking responsibility for preserving the veneer of "niceness" that I almost forgot to take responsibility for myself.) In conversations with men, we do almost all the work: sociologists have observed that in male-female social interactions it's the woman who throws out leading questions and verbal encouragements ("So how did you *feel* about that?" and so on) while the man, typically, says "Hmmmm." Wherever we go, we're perpetually smiling—the on-cue smile, like the now-outmoded curtsy, being one of our culture's little rituals of submission. We're trained to feel embarrassed if we're praised, but if we see a criticism coming at us from miles down the road, we rush to acknowledge it. And when we're feeling aggressive or angry or resentful, we just tighten up our smiles or turn them into rueful little pouts. In short, we spend a great deal of time acting like wimps.

For contrast, think of the macho stars we love to watch. Think, for example, of Mel Gibson facing down punk marauders in "The Road Warrior" … John Travolta swaggering his way through the early scenes of "Saturday Night Fever" … or Marlon Brando shrugging off the local law in "The Wild One." Would they simper their way through tight spots? Chatter aimlessly to keep the conversation going? Get all clutched up whenever they think they might—just might—have hurt someone's feelings? No, of course not, and therein, I think, lies their fascination for us.

The attraction of the "tough guy" is that he has—or at least seems to have—what most of us lack, and that is an aura of power and control. In an article, feminist psychiatrist Jean Baker Miller writes that "a Woman's using self-determined power for herself is equivalent to selfishness [and] destructiveness"—an equation that makes us want to avoid even the appearance of power. Miller cites cases of women who get depressed just when they're on the verge of success—and of women who do succeed and then bury their achievement in self-deprecation. As an example, she describes one company's periodic meetings to recognize outstanding salespeople: when a woman is asked to say a few words about her achievement, she tends to say something like, "Well, I really don't know how it happened. I guess I was just lucky this time." In contrast, the men will cheerfully own up to the hard work, intelligence, and so on, to which they owe their success. By putting herself down, a woman avoids feeling brazenly powerful and potentially "selfish"; she also does the traditional lady's work of trying to make everyone else feel better ("She's not really so smart, after all, just lucky").

So we might as well get a little tougher. And a good place to start is by cutting back on the small acts of deference that we've been programmed to perform since girlhood. Like unnecessary smiling. For many women—waitresses, flight attendants, receptionists—smiling is an occupational requirement, but there's no reason for anyone to go around grinning when she's not being paid for it. I'd suggest that we save our off-duty smiles for when we truly feel like sharing them, and if you're not sure what to do with your face in the meantime, study Clint Eastwood's expressions—both of them.

Along the same lines, I think women should stop taking responsibility for every human interaction we engage in. In a social encounter with a woman, the average man can go 25 minutes saying nothing more than "You don't say?" "Izzat so?" and, of course, "Hmmmm." Why should we do all the work? By taking so much responsibility for making conversations go well, we act as if we had much more at stake in the encounter than the other party—and that gives him (or her) the power advantage. Every now and then, we deserve to get more out of a

conversation than we put into it: I'd suggest not offering information you'd rather not share ("I'm really terrified that my sales plan won't work") and not, out of sheer politeness, soliciting information you don't really want ("Wherever did you get that lovely tie?"). There will be pauses, but they don't have to be awkward for *you*.

Is it true that some, perhaps most, men will interpret any decrease in female deference as a deliberate act of hostility. Omit the free smiles and perky conversation-boosters and someone is bound to ask, "Well, what's come over *you* today?" For most of us, the first impulse is to stare at our feet and make vague references to a terminally ill aunt in Atlanta, but we should have as much right to be taciturn as the average (male) taxi driver. If you're taking a vacation from smiles and small talk and some fellow is moved to inquire about what's "bothering" you, just stare back levelly and say, the international debt crisis, the arms race, or the death of God.

There are all kinds of ways to toughen up and potentially move up at work, and I leave the details to the purveyors of assertiveness training. But Jean Baker Miller's study underscores a fundamental principle that anyone can master on her own. We can stop acting less capable than we actually are. For example, in the matter of taking credit when credit is due, there's a key difference between saying "I was just lucky" and saying "I had a plan and it worked." If you take the credit you deserve, you're letting people know that you were confident you'd succeed all along, and that you fully intend to do so again.

Finally, we may be able to learn something from men about what to do with anger. As a general rule, women get irritated: men get angry. We make tight little smiles of ladylike exasperation; they pound on desks and roar. I wouldn't recommend emulating the full basso profundo male tantrum, but women do need ways of expressing justified anger clearly, colourfully, and, when necessary, crudely. If you're not just irritated, but *pissed off*, it might help to say so.

I, for example, have rerun the scene with the prestigious professor many times in my mind. And in my mind, I play it like Eastwood. I start by moving my chair over to where I can look the professor full in the face. I let him do the chattering, and when it becomes evident that he has nothing serious to say, I lean back and cross my arms, just to let him know that he's wasting my time. I do not smile, neither do I nod encouragement. Nor, of course, do I respond to his blandishments with apologetic shrugs and blushes. Then, at the first flicker of lechery, I stand up and announce coolly, "All right, I've had enough of this crap." Then I walk out—slowly, deliberately, confidently. Just like a man.

Or—now that I think of it—just like a woman.

READING COMPREHENSION

■ Indicate if each statement is true (T) or false (F) according to the reading.

1. _____ Ehrenreich believed for years that women should always act very ladylike.

2. _____ Ehrenreich is willing to admit that what women could learn from men is how to get tough.

3. _____ According to Ehrenreich, women spend a great deal of time acting like a beautiful princess.

4. _____ Jean Baker Miller asserts that women avoid feeling powerful and

selfish by putting themselves down.

5. _____ Ehrenreich recommends women should stop unnecessary smiling

and offering information you'd rather not share.

■ Discuss the following questions with your classmates.

1. Ehrenreich contrasts "being touch" and "being ladylike."

Do you think her description of a lady is fair?

2. For what major purposes does Ehrenreich quote Jean Baker Miller's study?

3. There are no positive examples of male character in the essay.

We know that a good man is not tough, aggressive, and violent.

What characteristics does a good man possess?

4. From your point of view, what kind of attitude would be desirable for

women to assume?

Culture

24 Why Boys Don't Play with Dolls

by Katha Pollitt

It's twenty-eight years since the founding of now, and boys still like trucks and girls still like dolls. Increasingly, we are told that the source of these robust preferences must lie outside society—in prenatal hormonal influences, brain chemistry, genes—and that feminism has reached its natural limits. What else could possibly explain the love of preschool girls for party dresses or the desire of toddler boys to own more guns than Mark from Michigan?

True, recent studies claim to show small cognitive differences between the sexes: He gets around by orienting himself in space; she does it by remembering landmarks. Time will tell if any deserve the hoopla with which each is invariably greeted, over the protests of the researchers themselves. But even if the results hold up (and the history of such research is not encouraging), we don't need studies of sex-differentiated brain activity in reading, say, to understand why boys and girls still seem so unalike.

The feminist movement has done much for some women, and something for every woman, but it has hardly turned America into a playground free of sex roles. It hasn't even got women to stop dieting or men to stop interrupting them.

Instead of looking at kids to "prove" that differences in behavior by sex are innate, we can look at the ways we raise kids as an index to how unfinished the feminist revolution really is, and how tentatively it is embraced even by adults who fully expect their daughters to enter previously male-dominated professions and their sons to change diapers.

I'm at a children's birthday party. "I'm sorry," one mom silently mouths to the mother of the birthday girl, who has just torn open her present—Tropical Splash Barbie. Now, you can love Barbie or you can hate Barbie, and there are feminists in both camps. But *apologize* for Barbie? Inflict Barbie, against your own convictions, on the child of a friend you know will be none too pleased?

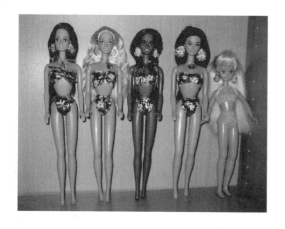

Every mother in that room had spent years becoming a person who had to be taken seriously, not least by herself. Even the most attractive, I'm willing to bet, had suffered over her body's failure to fit the impossible American ideal. Given all that, it seems crazy to transmit Barbie to the next generation. Yet to reject her is to say that what Barbie represents—being sexy, thin, stylish—is unimportant, which is obviously not true, and children know it's not true.

Women's looks matter terribly in this society, and so Barbie, however ambivalently, must be passed along. After all, there are worse toys. The Cut and Style Barbie styling head, for example, a grotesque object intended to encourage "hair play." The grown-ups who give that probably apologize, too.

How happy would most parents be to have a child who flouted sex conventions? I know a lot of women, feminists, who complain in a comical, eyeball-rolling way about their sons' passion for sports: the ruined weekends, obnoxious coaches, macho values. But they would not think of discouraging their sons from participating in this activity they find so foolish. Or do they? Their husbands are sports fans, too, and they like their husbands a lot.

Could it be that even sports-resistant moms see athletics as part of manliness? That if their sons wanted to spend the weekend writing up their diaries, or reading, or baking, they'd find it disturbing? Too anti-social? Too lonely? Too gay?

Theories of innate differences in behavior are appealing. They let parents off the hook—no small recommendation in a culture that holds moms, and sometimes even dads, responsible for their children's every misstep on the road to bliss and success.

They allow grown-ups to take the path of least resistance to the dominant culture, which always requires less psychic effort, even if it means more actual work: Just ask the working mother who comes home exhausted and nonetheless finds it easier to pick up her son's socks than make him do it himself. They let families buy for their children, without *too* much guilt, the unbelievably sexist junk that the kids, who have been watching commercials since birth, understandably crave.

But the thing the theories do most of all is tell adults that the *adult* world—in

which moms and dads still play by many of the old rules even as they question and fidget and chafe against them—is the way it's supposed to be. A girl with a doll and a boy with a truck "explain" why men are from Mars and women are from Venus, why wives do housework and husbands just don't understand.

The paradox is that the world of rigid and hierarchical sex roles evoked by determinist theories is already passing away. Three-year-olds may indeed insist that doctors are male and nurses female, even if their own mother is a physician. Six-year-olds know better. These days, something like half of all medical students are female, and male applications to nursing school are inching upward. When tomorrow's three-year-olds play doctor, who's to say how they'll assign the roles?

With sex roles, as in every area of life, people aspire to what is possible, and conform to what is necessary. But these are not fixed, especially today. Biological determinism may reassure some adults about their present, but it is feminism, the ideology of flexible and converging sex roles, that fits our children's future. And the kids, somehow, know this.

That's why, if you look carefully, you'll find that for every kid who fits a stereotype, there's another who's breaking one down. Sometimes it's the same kid—the boy who skateboards *and* takes cooking in his after-school program; the girl who collects stuffed animals *and* A-pluses in science.

Feminists are often accused of imposing their "agenda" on children. Isn't that what adults always do, consciously and unconsciously? Kids aren't born religious, or polite, or kind, or able to remember where they put their sneakers. Inculcating these behaviors, and the values behind them, is a tremendous amount of work, involving many adults. We don't have a choice, really, about *whether* we should give our children messages about what it means to be male and female—they're bombarded with them from morning till night.

The question, as always, is what do we want those messages to be?

READING COMPREHENSION

■ Indicate if each statement is true (T) or false (F) according to the reading.

1. _____ Pollitt says that we are told that the source of the continued preference of boys for trucks and girls for dolls lie outside society.

2. _____ Pollitt is satisfied with the recent studies which show small cognitive differences between the sexes.

3. _____ The writer agrees with biological determinism which means our behavior is innate and makes it possible to separate traditional male and female sex roles.

4. _____ According to Pollitt, the world of rigid, hierarchical sex roles is at an end.

5. _____ Pollitt argues that feminism as the ideology of flexible and converging sex roles fits our children's future.

■ Discuss the following questions with your classmates

1. Pollitt makes an argument that while in principle most parents might reject our society's sex-role conventions, in practice they do not want their children to flout them. What does it mean?

2. Pollitt clearly argues against a deterministic view of sex roles.
   Do you agree with her ideas? Why or why not?

3. Stereotypes can be positive or negative.
   Do you have a sexual stereotype of yourself?

4. The sexual stereotyping of men and women has a profound impact on our society. Sex roles are changing at work and at home. How have changes in sex roles affected the structures of families and the lives of their members in Korea?

25 A Chinese Reporter on Cape Cod

by GUAN KEGUANG

Next to the newsroom in the *Cape Cod Times* main office building there is a "lunchroom." My colleagues and I sometimes go there to buy something to eat or drink from the vending machines.

The experience has been quite a novelty for me. I put in some coins, push a button, and out comes what I want.

The machines offer a variety of food and drinks. Many of them are new to me and the labels don't tell me much about what's inside. The operation is simple and automatic. But so many decisions!

Such a process epitomizes what I have experienced while struggling hard to adapt my traditional ways of thinking and doing things to an American environment, which demands constantly considering alternatives and making decisions.

This has been no easy job for me.

For almost half a century I have lived in a culture where choices and decisions are made by authorities and circumstances rather than by individuals and personal preferences.

It's OK for young children to have things arranged for them by their parents, because they are inexperienced in life and not wise enough to make important decisions. But when they reach their late teens they don't like to be treated that way—even in China. They yearn for independence and freedom, as the recent demonstrations have shown. They are frustrated when things don't go their way and they find themselves helpless and unable to do anything about their fate.

When the time comes to enter the work force, however, reality sets in. They are assigned a job, and that's it. Moreover, the job assignment determines where you must live.

If you have completed twelve years' schooling, but you fail in the college entrance examination and are not admitted, the government will assign you a job perhaps as a factory worker, a store clerk, or a bus driver. Very likely that will be you lifelong job, because you can't freely pick and choose or change your job. Once you are in a job you will have to stick to it, unless the authorities want to transfer you to another job. You could negotiate with the authorities, but the government always has the final say.

Students do have an opportunity to state their preference among university and courses of study- and if you pass your exams with flying colors, with scores much higher than others, you will be admitted into a department of a university of your own choice. But once you get into a university you stay in your major for four or five years without a break. You do not change your major. You take the courses given to you, pass all the exams, behave well and toe the party line, earn your bachelor's degree and graduate.

Then, you just wait until a job is assigned to you. During the waiting period, students with "connections" seek to influence the decision. A few succeed. In any event, until the decision is made, you will not know where you will go and what your lifelong career will be.

Your job assignment notice is more than a certificate with which you report for duty. It is also a certificate for your residence registration and your daily necessity rations. If you don't like the job assigned to you and refuse to take it, you are jobless. Because you don't have an official permission to live in any place other than where the job is, you won't get your ration coupons.

Your choice, therefore, is very simple: to eat or not to eat.

Every graduate is guaranteed a job. Each job affords the same starting salary. Engineer, schoolteacher, office clerk, truck driver, scientist—the difference in salary is negligible. That is the socialist way.

No matter if you like it or not, you stay with your job.

No matter if you liked or not, you stay with your job.

If you are not very ambitious, life can be very easy for you. Its pace won't be so maddeningly fast as it is here in America. You don't have to worry about choosing alternatives or making decisions. You don't have to worry about getting laid off.

Since you don't have much to choose from and everything is panned and arranged for you, you will be better off if you take things easy. As an old Chinese saying goes: "Those who are content are forever happy."

People like that—who have been content to let their decisions be made for them would find it hard to get used to the American lifestyle, to keep their eyes open to opportunities, to be searching constantly for a better job, a better place to

live. Such a way of life would be too risky, too precarious, too challenging.

Our old tradition taught us to be humble, modest, unassuming, moderate and passive. Even when a Chinese host treats a guest to a dinner consisting of twelve courses and costing half of his monthly salary, he still apologizes repeatedly to the guest between the courses for the "inadequate" meal he has prepared for his honorable guest. Meanwhile, the guest politely and humbly refuses to accept the food his host keeps piling up on his dish, because he feels he shouldn't assume that he deserves so much good food and he should leave more good stuff for the host family, even though he is very hungry at the moment and he likes the food immensely.

The other day while I was going through the classified ads in the magazine *Editor & Publisher*, I came across ads placed by publications in search of "aggressive, talented, hungry" reporters.

What could I do if I wanted such a position?

If I were hungry, I would try every face-saving means not to admit it.

If I were talented, I would (or should) be modest enough not to advertise it.

Even if I were desperately in need of the position, I still wouldn't know how to be aggressive. I wonder if I should take a crash course, teaching me how to be aggressive, talented, and hungry.

READING COMPREHENSION

■ Indicate if each statement is true (T) or false (F) according to the reading.

1. _____ Guan regards American vending machines as extraordinary.

2. _____ For almost half a century Guan has lived in a culture where choices

   are made by authorities.

3. _____ Guan had a fun time adjusting to American life style.

4. _____ Guan mentions that Chinese allow to choose their job.

■ Discuss the following questions with your classmates.

1. What is Guan's job in this essay?

2. Do you think Guan is overreacting when he describes aspects of American life?

3. Why don't you compare your lifestyle with Chinese's in this essay?

26 Entering the New World

by V.S. NAIPAUL

In the morning I was telephoned from the hotel lobby by a man called Ebony. He said he had heard from Busby that a writer was in Abidjan, and he had come to meet this writer. He, Ebony, was himself a poet.

I went down to see him. He was a cheerful young man of regal appearance, with the face of a Benin bronze, and he was regally attired, with a brightly patterned skullcap and a rich African tunic. He said the skullcap and tunic were from Volta. His family employed laborers from Volta and he had always, even as a child, liked their clothes.

He had been a journalist, he said, but he had given it up, because in the Ivory Coast journalism was like smoking: it could damage your health. He liked the joke; he made it twice. But he was vague about the journalism he had done. He said he was now a government servant, in the department of the environment. He had written a paper on thing that might be done environmentally in the Ivory Coast. But after twelve months he had heard nothing about his paper. So now he just went to the office and from time to time he wrote poetry.

He said, "I have a theory about African administrations. But it is difficult and will take too long to tell you."

He had come to see me—and the hotel was a good way out of the town—because he was sociable; because he wanted to practice his English; and because, as a poet and intellectual, he wanted to try out his ideas.

I offered coffee. he offered me a cola nut, the African token of friendship. I nibbled at my grubby, purple-skinned nut: bitter. He chewed his zestfully, giving little dry spits of chewed husk to his left and right, and then at the end of his chew taking out the remainder of the husk with his fingers and placing it on the ashtray.

He asked why I had come to the Ivory Coast. I said because it was successful and French.

He said, "Charlemagne wasn't my ancestor."

I felt it had been said before, and not only by Ebony. He ran on to another idea. "The French run countries like pigsties. They believe that the sole purpose of men is to eat, to go to the toilet, and to sleep." So the French colonialists created bourgeois people. Bourgeois? "The bourgeois want peace, order. The bourgeois can fit into any political system, once they have peace. On the other hand, the British colonialists created entrepreneurs." Entrepreneurs? "Entrepreneurs want to change things." Entrepreneurs were revolutionaries.

Antithesis, balance: the beauty rather than the validity of a thought: I thought I could detect his French training. I began to examine his ideas of the bourgeois and the entrepreneur, but he didn't encourage me. He said, playfully, it was only an idea. Starting on another cola nut—he had a handful in his tunic pocket—he said, "Africans live at peace with nature. Europeans want to conquer or dominate nature." That was familiar to me. I had heard similar words from young Muslim fundamentalists in Malaysia: Ecological, Western romance bouncing back like a corroborating radio signal from remote, inactive worlds, But that again was an idea Ebony didn't want to stay with.

Ebony said, "I saw white men for the first time when I was fourteen of fifteen, when I went to school. That was the first time I discovered the idea of racial superiority. African children are trained not to look elders in the eye. It is disrespectful. At school the French teachers took this to be a sign of African hypocrisy."

What was the point of this story?

Ebony said, "So I thought my French teachers inferior."

I felt this racial story, with its triumphant twist, had previously had a sympathetic foreign listener. And it turned out that there was a Scandinavian woman journalist who had made a great hit with Ebony, She was now in Spain and Ebony earnestly asked me—two or three times—to look her up and pass on his regards.

Ebony said, "When my father sent me to the school, do you know what he said? He said, 'Remember. I am not sending you to the school to be a white man or a Frenchman. I am sending you to enter the new world, that's all.'"

I felt that in his own eyes Ebony had done that. ... Ebony said he had no money, no car. The salary he got from the government was less than the rent he paid. He had come to the hotel on his bicycle. But I thought he was relaxed, a whole man. He knew where he was, how he had got there, and he liked the novelty of what he saw. There was no true anxiety behind his scattered ideas. At any rate he was less anxious than a romantic or concerned outsider might have wished him to be. Ideas about Africa, words, poetry, meeting foreigners—all this was part of his relishing of life, part of his French-inspired role as intellectual, part of the new world he had happily entered.

He went away on his bicycle, and I took a taxi later to a beach restaurant at the other end of the city, beyond the industrial and port area. The lunch there, and the French style of the place were usually worth the fare and the journey in the midday heat through the traffic and the crowds. But today it wasn't so.

It was more than a matter of an off day. The waiters, impeccable the day before, were casual, vacant. There were long delays, mistakes, some of the portions were absurdly small; the bill, when it came, was wrong. Someone was missing, perhaps the French or European manager. And with him more than good service had gone: the whole restaurant idea had vanished. An elaborate organization had collapsed. The waiters—Ivorian: these jobs were lucrative—seemed to have forgotten, from one day to the next, why they were doing what they did. And their faces seemed to have altered as well. They were not waiters now, in spite of their flowered tunics. Their faces and manners radiated various degrees of tribal authority. I saw them as men of weight in the village: witch doctors, herbalists, men who perhaps put on masks and did the sacred dances. The true life was there, in the mysteries of the village. The restaurant, with its false, arbitrary ritual, was the charade: I half began to see it so.

Ebony had been told by his father: "I am not sending you to the school to become a white man. I am sending you to enter the new world."

The new world existed in the minds of other men. Remove those men, and their ideas—which after all had no finality—would disappear. Skills could be taught. What was fragile—to men whose complete, real life lay in another realm of the spirit—was faith in the new world.

■ Indicate if each statement is true (T) or false (F) according to the reading.

1. _____ Ebony commented on French versus British colonies.

2. _____ Ebony faced the conflict between native and European influences.

3. _____ Naipaul comments about fragility of worlds that exist mainly

    in someone's mind.

4. _____ Ebony mentions that the French run countries democratically.

■ Discuss the following questions with your classmates.

1. Have you ever eaten in a restaurant, a store, where you unexpectedly

    became aware of the "real" life someone waiting on you?

2. Do you agree with Ebony's comment, "the British colonists created

    entrepreneurs"?

3. This essay depicts Africans living in former European colonies.

    What qualities make up a traditional African consciousness or character?

27 Bumps and Personalities

by Milada Broukal

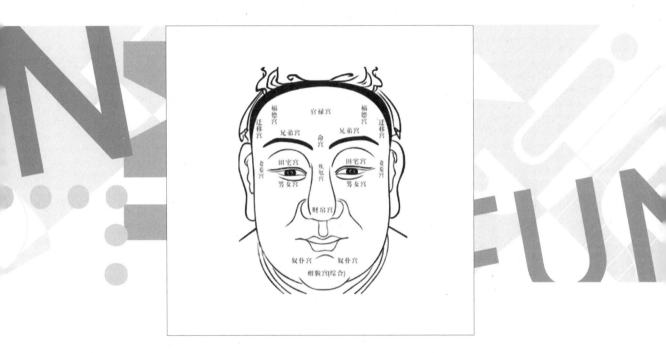

Have you ever been afraid of or attracted to someone just because of the way the person looks? When you first meet someone, it is not unusual to react to his/her appearance. But these are first impressions, and most people assume that it takes time to find out what someone is really like. It is possible, however, that a person's appearance reveals more than we realize. According to some experts, a person's face, head, and body can reveal a great deal about personality.

Since ancient times, people have practiced the art of physiognomy, or reading character from physical features. The ancient Greeks compared the human face to the faces of various animals and birds, such as the eagle and the horse. They believed people shared certain character traits with the animals they resembled. A person with an equine, or horselike, face was thought to be loyal, brave, and stern. A person with an aquiline, or eaglelike, nose was believed to be bold and courageous, as well as arrogant and self-centered.

Physiognomists study such features as the shape of the head, the length and thickness of the neck, the color and thickness of the hair, and the shape of the nose, mouth, eyes, and chin. They believe that round-faced people are self-confident. Prominent cheekbones show strength of character, while a pointed nose reveals curiosity. Heavy, arched eyebrows belong to a decisive individual, while thin, arched eyebrows signal a restless and active personality. Almond-shaped eyes reveal an artistic nature. Round, soft eyes belong to dreamers. Down-turned lips reveal a proud character, while a long, pointed chin indicates someone who likes to give orders.

A related—though not as ancient—art is phrenology, the study of the bumps on the head. Phrenologists have identified forty bumps of various shapes and sizes on the human head. They "read" these bumps to identify a person's talents and character. For example, a bump between the nose and forehead is said to be present in people who have natural elegance and a love of beauty. A bump behind the curve of the ear is the sign of a courageous and adventurous person.

Phrenologists are not so much interested in health as they are in character and personality. They believe, for example, that a bulge in the center of the forehead is typical of people who have a good memory and a desire for knowledge. A small bump at the top of the head indicates a person who has strong moral character, while a bump just below this one is a sign of generosity and a kind, good nature. Phrenologists say a bump just above the tip of the eyebrow is

found in people who love order and discipline, and a rise at the very back of the head is evident in people who are very attached to their families.

Phrenology was developed in the early eighteenth century by Franz Joseph Gall, a doctor in Vienna. His interest began at school when he noticed that boys with prominent eyes seemed to have the best memories. This led him to believe that a connection existed between appearance and ability. Dr. Gall's research interested many people, but he was ridiculed by other doctors. When he died in 1828, he was a poor and bitter man. It was only many years later that Dr. Gall's theories found support among some doctors and scientists, and today the art of phrenology is still popular.

READING COMPREHENSION

■ Indicate if each statement is true (T) or false (F) according to the reading.

1. _____ Physiognomy is a modern practice.

2. _____ The ancient Greeks compared the human face to those of animals.

3. _____ A bump on the forehead is a sign of courage.

4. _____ Physiognomists study the shape of the head, face, and body.

5. _____ Dr. Gall's research did not interest many people.

■ Discuss the following questions with your classmates.

1. Why did the Greeks compare humans to animals?

2. Why did other doctors ridicule Dr. Gall's research?

3. What might a physiognomist say about someone with a long nose, thin eyebrows, and almond-shaped eyes?

4. According to your astrological sign, what character traits are you supposed to have? Do you fit the description?

5. Do you think that astrology is more precise than physiognomy or phrenology?

28 Cultural Attitudes towards Time

by Lawrence J. Zwier & Lynn Stafford-Yilmaz

Culture is a society's system of shared ideas about how the world works and how people should act. Each person's culture has a great influence on how he or she behaves and interprets the world. Some cultural anthropologists even think that culture is a kind of template for our thinking and feelings. That is, they think that culture actually helps create our thoughts and emotions, just as DNA creates our bodies. Among these basic culture-influenced aspects of life is a sense of time.

According to anthropologist Irving Hallowell, there is no evidence that humans have an inborn sense of time. A person's temporal concepts are probably determined largely by culture. One study showed that infants, after a few days of listening to speech around them, will move their heads and limbs in rhythm with the speech they hear. As children develop, they adapt more fully to their temporal culture. This temporal culture influences language, music, poetry and dance. It also affects relationships. We tend to get along well with people who share our sense of time.

One type of cultural attitude towards time is found in polychronic cultures. Some Mediterranean and southwest Asian cultures are usually placed in this category. Such cultures emphasize relationships among people, flexible timing of appointments, and the careful completion of processes rather than strict schedules. Polychronic people seldom feel that time is being wasted. They tend to consider each activity valuable on its own, not just as part of a larger process.

Polychronic people tend to have many projects going on at the same time, and they may shift frequently from one task to another. They change plans often. For polychronic people, work time is not clearly separable from personal time, so business meetings are considered a form of socializing.

Monochronic cultures, on the other hand, are oriented towards tasks and schedules. Cultures usually considered monochronic can be found in northern Europe, North America, and some parts of eastern Asia.

Monochronic people feel that time is tangible and inflexible and that "time is money." They do one thing at a time and concentrate on each thing in sequence. Time and job commitments are very important to them and they tend to follow plans rigidly. Also, monochronic people clearly separate their work and personal time, and they place a high value on privacy.

As you might expect, people from polychronic and monochronic cultures often misunderstand each other because of their different senses of time. For example, because a monochronic culture is highly compartmentalized,

monochronic people tend to sequence conversations as well as tasks. They would not, for instance, interrupt a phone call in order to greet another person who just came into the room. In contrast, polychronic people are comfortable with having multiple conversations at the same time. They would consider it rude not to greet someone entering during the phone conversation.

The effects of time-related cultural differences are very apparent in the business world. As Edward and Mildred Hall, prominent temporal-culture researchers, have noted, many millions of dollars have been lost because of such differences. Being late to an appointment or taking a long time to get down to business is normal in polychronic cultures. In monochronic cultures, such behavior makes a business person seem unreliable or even rude. Countless cross-cultural business deals have fallen apart because of misunderstandings about temporal culture.

Of course, we have to be careful when we generalize about cultures. Human beings are very diverse creatures, and cultures accommodate a wide range of behaviors. Within a fast-paced culture, a large number of slow-paced people survive perfectly well. Within slow-paced cultures, faster-paced individuals can find their own niche. A cultural generalization is a statement about what is typical, not about what always happens.

READING COMPREHENSION

■ Indicate if each statement is true (T) or false (F) according to the reading.

1. _____ Humans are born with a natural sense of time.

2. _____ Babies move to the speed of speech around them.

3. _____ A polychronic culture is faster-paced than a monochronic culture.

4. _____ Everyone within a given culture has the same temporal sense.

5. _____ Meetings between monochronic people are likely to be direct and focused on a single task.

■ Discuss the following questions with your classmates.

1. How might people from monochronic or polychronic cultures view schedules?

2. According to the reading, why have temporal differences among cultures cost millions of dollars?

3. In this article the author mentions that "cultures accommodate a wide range of behaviors." Do you agree with the author? Why or why not?

4. Talk about the reasons why we have to be careful when we generalize about cultures.

29 Why I Want a Wife

by Judy Syfers Brady

I belong to that classification of people known as wives. I am A Wife. And, not altogether incidentally, I am a mother.

Not too long ago a male friend of mine appeared on the scene fresh from a recent divorce. He had one child, who is, of course, with his ex-wife. He is looking for another wife. As I thought about him while I was ironing one evening, it suddenly occurred to me that I, too, would like to have a wife. Why do I want a wife?

I would like to go back to school so that I can become economically independent, support myself, and, if need be, support those dependent upon me. I want a wife who will work and send me to school. And while I am going to school I want a wife to take care of my children. I want a wife to keep track of the children's doctor and dentist appointments. And to keep track of mine, too. I want a wife to make sure my children eat properly and are kept clean. I want a wife who will wash the children's clothes and keep them mended. I want a wife who is a good nurturing attendant to my children, who arranges for their schooling, makes sure that they have an adequate social life with their peers, takes them to the park, the zoo, etc. I want a wife who takes care of the children when they are sick, a wife who arranges to be around when the children need special care, because, of course, I cannot miss classes at school. My wife must arrange to lose time at work and not lose the job. It may mean a small cut in my wife's income from time to time, but I guess I can tolerate that. Needless to say, my wife will arrange and pay for the care of the children while my wife is working.

I want a wife who will take care of *my* physical needs. I want a wife who will keep my house clean. A wife who will pick up after my children, a wife who will pick up after me. I want a wife who will keep my clothes clean, ironed, mended, replaced when need be, and who will see to it that my personal things are kept in their proper place so that I can find what I need the minute I need it. I want a wife who cooks the meals, a wife who is a good cook. I want a wife who will plan the menus, do the necessary grocery shopping, prepare the meals, serve them pleasantly, and then do the cleaning up while I do my studying. I want a wife who will care for me when I am sick and sympathize with my pain and loss of time from school. I want a wife to go along when our family takes a vacation so that someone can continue to care for me and my children when I need a rest and change of scene.

I want a wife who will not bother me with rambling complaints about a wife's duties. But I want a wife who will listen to me when I feel the need to explain a

rather difficult point I have come across in my course of studies. And I want a wife who will type my papers for me when I have written them.

I want a wife who will take care of the details of my social life. When my wife and I are invited out by my friends, I want a wife who will take care of the baby-sitting arrangements. When I meet people at school that I like and want to entertain, I want a wife who will have the house clean, will prepare a special meal, serve it to me and my friends, and not interrupt when I talk about the things that interest me and my friends. I want a wife who will have arranged that the children are fed and ready for bed before my guests arrive so that the children do not bother us. I want a wife who takes care of the needs of my guests so that they feel comfortable, who makes sure that they have an ashtray, that they are passed the hors d'oeuvres, that they are offered a second helping of the food, that their wine glasses are replenished when necessary, that their coffee is served to them as they like it. And I want a wife who knows that sometimes I need a night out by myself.

I want a wife who is sensitive to my sexual needs, a wife who makes love passionately and eagerly when I feel like it, a wife who makes sure that I am satisfied. And, of course, I want a wife who will not demand sexual attention when I am not in the mood for it. I want a wife who assumes the complete responsibility for birth control, because I do not want more children. I want a wife who will remain sexually faithful to me so that I do not have to clutter up my intellectual life with jealousies. And I want a wife who understands that my sexual needs may entail more than strict adherence to monogamy. I must, after all, be able to relate to people as fully as possible.

If, by chance, I find another person more suitable as a wife than the wife I already have, I want the liberty to replace my present wife with another one. Naturally, I will expect a fresh, new life; my wife will take the children and be solely responsible for them so that I am left free.

When I am through with school and have a job, I want my wife to quit working and remain at home so that my wife can more fully and completely take care of a wife's duties.

My God, who *wouldn't* want a wife?

READING COMPREHENSION

■ Indicate if each statement is true (T) or false (F) according to the reading.

1. _____ The reason why the author wants a wife was that she met someone from the same high school who just got married in the high school reunion.

2. _____ In this essay the author puts her focus on the important roles of husband.

3. _____ The author admires promising roles of mother/wife with a little bit of help from the spouse.

4. _____ The author regrets not finishing the university studies.

■ Discuss the following questions with your classmates.

1. In your country, what kind of roles are expected to wives?

2. Why do you think the author wants a wife?
   What kind of wife does the author want to have?

3. Do you want to have a wife? Why or why not?

4. Do you want to have a husband? Why or why not?

30 Tonic Water, Please

by Tetsuya Saruhashi

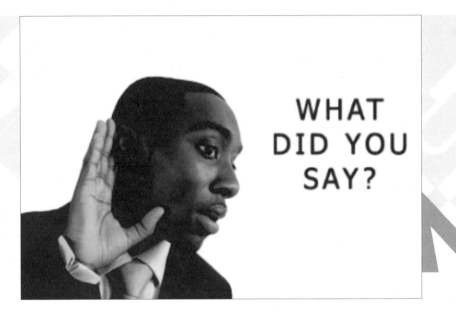

How well do you speak English? Could you survive in an English-speaking country? Last year I went to live and study in Canada. Before going, I took several English conversation classes. I also listened to a lot of English conversation tapes and I practiced speaking English with some foreign friends in my country. But could I communicate with people in Canada?

During my first months in Canada, I didn't have a lot of trouble understanding people. This was a happy surprise. Unfortunately, however, Canadians couldn't always understand me. This was because of my pronunciation.

My biggest pronunciation problems were with the "v" sound and the "r" sound. For example, when I said the word *vote*, it sounded like *bote*. And when I said the word *rate*, it sounded like *late*. One day I decided to look for some volunteer work. I went to the tourist center in Toronto to ask for information about volunteering.

"Can I help you?" the woman at the tourist center asked.

"Yes, I'm looking for some volunteer work," I replied. Unfortunately, I pronounced the word *volunteer* like *borunteer*. "I'm sorry," she said, "What are you looking for?"

"Volunteer work," I answered, saying *borunteer* again. She looked at me strangely and then she called to a man behind the counter.

"Can I help you?" the man asked.

"Yes, I'm looking for some volunteer work," I repeated.

"Could you write that for me?" he asked. I wrote the words down and he immediately understood me. After that, I spent a lot of time practicing the "*v*" sound and the "*r*" sound.

I had trouble pronouncing a few other English sounds, too. I remember a funny experience I had at a night club. I wanted to get something to drink, so I went up to the bartender.

"Excuse me, tonic water, please," I said.

"What?" the bartender asked.

I asked, "Can I have a tonic water?"

"Say it again," he responded.

I was kind of disappointed that he couldn't understand me. I repeated my request several times, but still he couldn't understand me. Then, suddenly, he

opened the cash register and took out some quarters. He put the quarters on the bar and began to count them. At first, I didn't know what he was doing. Then, suddenly, I understood. I asked for tonic water, but he thought I asked for "twenty quarters"!

I burst into laughter and said, "No, I didn't ask for twenty quarters. I just want tonic water."

The bartender seemed embarrassed. "I'm so sorry," he said to me. "The music is so loud."

Now, whenever I ask for tonic water, I remember this incident and I look forward to the bartender's response.

READING COMPREHENSION

■ Indicate if each statement is true (T) or false (F) according to the reading.

1. _____ Tetsuya Saruhashi studied English before he traveled to Canada.

2. _____ He couldn't understand English speakers when they talked to him.

3. _____ Some Canadians couldn't understand Tetsuya when he spoke English.

4. _____ Tetsuya had trouble pronouncing words with the "v" sound.

5. _____ Tetsuya asked the bartender at the night club for money.

■ Discuss the following questions with your classmates.

1. What pronunciation problems do you have when you speak English?

2. What pronunciation problems do foreigners have when they speak your language? Think of one or more examples.

3. Do you think you should study English pronunciation? Why or why not?

4. Can you think of any effective ways to improve your English pronunciation? If you can, list all your ideas.